Artstarts

Artstarts

Drama, Music, Movement, Puppetry, and Storytelling Activities

MARTHA BRADY

PATSY T. GLEASON

1994

TEACHER IDEAS PRESS

A Division of
Libraries Unlimited, Inc.
Englewood, Colorado

To my mother, who gave me permission to always be me.
M.D.B.

TEACHER IDEAS PRESS
A Division of
Libraries Unlimited, Inc.
P.O. Box 6633
Englewood, CO 80155-6633
1-800-237-6124

Project Editor: Louisa M. Griffin
Copy Editor: Tama Serfoss
Typesetter: Kay Minnis
Interior Book Design: Judy Gay Matthews

Library of Congress Cataloging-in-Publication Data

Brady, Martha.
    Artstarts : drama, music, movement, puppetry, and storytelling
activities / Martha Brady, Patsy T. Gleason.
    xii, 219 p. 22x28 cm.
    Includes bibliographical references (p. 213) and index.
    ISBN 1-56308-148-2
    1. Arts--Study and teaching (Elementary)--United States.
I. Gleason, Patsy T. (Patsy Timmerman) II. Title. III. Title: Art
starts.
NX303.A1B73   1994
372.13'32--dc20   93-36674
                                                        CIP

Contents

Acknowledgments

We wish to acknowledge every teacher we've ever had—good or bad, every student we've ever had—difficult or easy, and every colleague who has assisted us—knowingly or unknowingly. We thank you for your contribution to this book. We wish to acknowledge the students at the Telluride Schools, Telluride, Colorado, who squirmingly, smilingly, and creatively allowed us to try out these activities on them, and showed us that the human heart has many wonderful disguises. Thanks to the Northern Arizona University Block students—Brian, Jennifer, Vee Vee, Peggy, Maria, Karen, Kara, Linda, Vicki, Robin, Wynne, Jodi, Ann, Lanny, Shannon, Lisa, Jay, Stephanie, Lorraine, Kathleen, Lilia, Bobbi, Joyce, Aileen, Susan, Cindy, Stacey, Tammy, Ann, Corina, Shanna, Julie, Tammy, Carole, Beth, Jami, Marci, Laura, Barbara, Sharlene, and Becky—for letting us include some of their original puppet scripts and song lyrics. We would like to thank Shawn Satterthwaite and Kathy Rovey, who took our music and cleaned it up. A special thanks to Don Boswell and Partners, who illustrated our chapter headings with such warm whimsy, and to the other authors, artists, and creative specialists, too numerous to mention, whose activities and ideas we used as catalysts for our own in this book. We acknowledge your dedication, your energy, and your commitment to the belief that the arts are, in fact, the universal glue.

Introduction

Lon Chaney, a popular actor in the 1920s and 1930s, was known as "The Man with a Thousand Faces" for his ability to play a multitude of different characters. We teachers have a lot in common with Mr. Chaney. We may not be called upon to portray the Hunchback of Notre Dame, but certainly during a typical school year we will play mother, father, big brother, and big sister to our students. At times we will become doctor, nurse, banker, minister, confessor, protector, and comedian to the children in our classes. We will be good guy and bad guy, stranger and friend, and in the midst of all these different roles, we must also find time to be teacher—just teacher.

Of course, being "just a teacher" often means wearing a thousand faces. Being just a teacher is a tough job. In fact, some consider teaching the toughest job there is. It drains us physically. It saps us mentally. It burns us up, and, unfortunately, it can burn us out. If, however, we teach because we love to, we rebound, we reenergize, and we continue to put on yet another face. Hopefully, using this book will help you rebound and reenergize with more vitality, and to wear all those different faces successfully.

We are committed to the belief that the integration of the creative arts into a regular elementary school curriculum provides students with a sense of self-discovery through the stimulation of all the senses. It empowers them to understand who they are at a deeper level through a clear acknowledgment of their whole persona. It allows them to choose how they learn. It can instill in them a much clearer definition of "wholeness."

For you, the teacher, the integration of the arts in the classroom will require you to stretch. It will require you to look at the different kinds of learners in your care. It will help you understand that skills, concepts, and content can be presented in different, but meaningful ways, using the child's own love for and sometimes hidden expertise in the creative arts. As with the student, it can reacquaint you with the definition of what makes us human.

What, then, are creative arts? Are they concerts at Carnegie Hall? An opera at the New York Met? Are they impressionistic paintings at the Guggenheim Museum or a watercolor at the Museum of Modern Art? Are they musical works on Broadway, a production of the *Nutcracker Suite* at the Kennedy Center? The creative arts are all of these. And more.

They are also a third grade Christmas play, a five-year-old's finger painting of a dog, a first grade class moving as autumn leaves, and a second grade class singing "Old MacDonald Had a Farm." The creative arts are storytelling, pantomime, movement, puppetry, music, and all those other happenings that move the body and the spirit. They are truly the energy of the heart.

The creative arts activities we have written and collected over the years are simple and straightforward. So is the format of this book. Each activity gives a recommended grade level, although most can be adapted for any age. Each provides a list of materials, an estimated time needed for each activity, and a statement of purpose so you will know the goal of the exercise. The procedures are written in sequential steps, clear and easy to understand. Academic variations are offered. And finally, there is the "Flourishes" section at the end of each exercise. These Flourishes are ways of showing how different and interesting ideas can come from one simple one.

Why did we write this book? First, we believe wholeheartedly that there is a place in everyone's life for the arts and we believe that there must be a place for the arts in the classroom. Second, as elementary schoolteachers ourselves, we know that there are never enough hours in the day for everything we must accomplish with our students. This book makes the inclusion of the arts possible. It relieves some of the fear associated with implementing arts activities, and saves prep time.

The most important reason for writing this book can be illustrated by recounting a recent experience we had. We were assisting one of our college students with a pantomime performance being presented by a fifth grade class with whom she was working. The students had had little experience in performance and none in pantomime. At the conclusion of the presentation, we bent down in front of a rumpled little girl whose face was covered with clown white and asked her, "What was the very best thing about what you just did today?" She looked up at us, grinned, and said, "It made my heart smile."

This is why we wrote the book. It made our hearts smile. Here's hoping it brings a smile to your heart and to your thousand faces as well.

Chapter 1

WARM-UPS

warm (wȯrm) adj. 1: heated 2: having heat in a moderate degree.

up (up) *adv.* 1: a direction 2: from a lower to a higher level.

warm-up (wȯrm up) *n.* 1: a prepatory activity. 2: a sweat suit 3: what pitchers do to their arms to prepare for a baseball game 4: first thing you do in class every morning 5: a way to get the blood pumping in your students 6: fun.

Warm-ups are nothing more than short exercises or activities, three or four minutes long, that allow a child to feel comfortable about a learning situation, whether or not it is creative arts. These short activities are like the little spoon of ice cream you sample at Baskin-Robbins before you select the triple-dip, double fudge sundae with marshmallows and bubble gum chunks. That is, warm-ups are the little slivers of taste that prepare students to get the most out of the main course.

Warm-ups do not necessarily need to directly connect with the content area you are about to introduce to the students. In other words, if you are going to work with multiplication, you don't need to do a math warm-up. It might be nice, however, to think of a warm-up that deals with rhythm and patterning. Patterning is a vital aspect of math, therefore a pattern-type activity would naturally work well in this situation. One such pattern-type activity is clap/response. It requires students to duplicate the pattern or rhythm the teacher makes by clapping hands.

Warm-ups can be used effectively anytime. At the beginning of the school day they are especially useful in focusing everyone's attention on the same subject. That may be reading, math, class rules, announcements, or whatever you do first each morning. A successful warm-up will prepare your class to actively engage that subject. They are also useful during the middle of a lesson when you see, by noise level or body language, that the students are not on your wavelength. Just stop what you are doing, regroup with a warm-up that everyone can succeed in, then, when everyone is back on track, proceed with the original lesson.

Let's say you are having one of those days. You know, the day when the lunch tickets get lost, one bus with half your students is 20 minutes late, and the mother who promised to teach the class quilt making for an hour forgets and goes bowling instead. You know. One of those days. Well, my friend, using warm-ups during those times when you are caught unprepared will keep your class engaged and productive.

You will also want to use warm-ups on those days when everything goes well, when you are unabashedly brilliant, when the students seem to have IQs that rival the Dow Jones Average, and when the lunch is not only good, but you deem it a rare privilege to eat turkey pom poms with salsa. On those days, treat yourself and your students to some fun warm-ups during the last 20 minutes of class. It's a nice reward. Sort of like buying a whole pound of jelly beans and picking out only the red ones to eat.

Body Puzzles

GRADE LEVEL: 1-6

MATERIALS: none

AREA: floor space

TIME NEEDED: 10 minutes

PURPOSE: To practice problem solving, to use creative expression, to demonstrate "parts of a whole," and to determine sequential order.

PROCEDURES:

1. Warm-up—Ask for a volunteer to lie down in the middle of the floor space, forming the first "piece" of the body puzzle. Ask the other children, one at a time, to decide the form their own body puzzle pieces will take. Connect their piece to the group until they have formed a single human puzzle.

2. Ask volunteers to solve problems using body puzzles. For example, the teacher will call out an equation, "5+2 = ." Five students will come to the center of the space and form an interlocking puzzle. The class will count the pieces. Two more students join the group. The class will now count all of the pieces. The teacher will say, "5+2 = ..." Group responds, "7."

ACADEMIC VARIATIONS:

Art: Ask half of the class to go to the center space and form a body puzzle and then freeze their shapes. Ask the other half of the class to draw, in an abstract way, what they see. Then have students switch roles.

Creative Writing: Ask students to look at their drawings (see art variation above), give them titles, and write poems or short stories about what they see.

Social Studies: The students, individually or in small groups, make their bodies into the shapes of various states. They must then connect to the other *body states* at the appropriate place for their state's location.

FLOURISHES:

Divide the class into groups of three. Give each group a piece of tagboard. Let them use tempera paint, watercolors, or crayons to draw something collectively. Allow the pictures to dry. (Be sure to put pressure on the sheets during the drying process so that they don't curl up.) Now have each group cut their picture into puzzle pieces. Put the pieces in an envelope. Write "What is it?" on the outside of the envelope, and stick the envelope onto a bulletin board relating to puzzles. Let your students solve the puzzles during free time.

Body Sentences

GRADE LEVEL: 3-6

MATERIALS: none

AREA: classroom

TIME NEEDED: 5 minutes

PURPOSE: To create a visual sentence, to work cooperatively, to use pantomime to describe a word.

PROCEDURES:

1. Divide students into groups of five or six. Each group will think of a short sentence. Each person in the group will be responsible for pantomiming one word in the sentence.

2. The students will stand side by side and act out, nonverbally, their word in the sentence. This pantomime can use body shapes and forms, gestures, or images. A sample sentence might be, "I love to read comics."

Student 1 (I)	will point to his or her eye.
Student 2 (love)	will flutter eyes while showing his or her heart beating.
Student 3 (to)	will hold up two fingers.
Student 4 (read)	will pretend to read a book.
Student 5 (comics)	will pretend to laugh.

ACADEMIC VARIATIONS:

Creative Writing: As a creative writing stimulus, ask several students to think of something to describe through pantomime, such as a tree, cloud, tornado, leg, and so on. These students will act out their definitions while the class tries to guess the word. Then the entire class will write poems or stories using all of the words.

Science: When reviewing vocabulary words, ask a group of students to go to the front of the class, decide on one science vocabulary word (e.g., *thermometer*), and use that word in a body sentence. The rest of the class must figure out not only the vocabulary word but the entire sentence as well.

Math: Ask a group to create a math equation using pantomime and shapes. The class must figure out the equation and solve it.

FLOURISHES:

To show the importance of individual differences, call out a sentence (e.g., "Rain makes me happy."). Students, individually and simultaneously, will create their own distinct body sentences. Point out interesting ways in which students solved the problem of how to define certain words in their sentence

Circle of Sounds

GRADE LEVEL: 1-6

MATERIALS: none

AREA: floor space

TIME NEEDED: 15 minutes

PURPOSE: To practice creative expression, to show the importance of individual differences, to enhance listening skills, to promote self-esteem.

PROCEDURES:

1. Direct the students to sit on the floor in a circle. Beginning with the teacher, and going around the circle, each person will repeat a sound.

   catsup coming out of a bottle
   creaking door
   a go-cart going around a racetrack

2. All together, the students will make the same sound in their own way, e.g.,

   an animal found in a pet store
   the wind
   a machine in a factory

3. One at a time, students go around the circle, look into the eyes of the person next to them, and repeat a phrase in as unique a manner as possible. Suggest they use different accents and emotions, such as that of a Texan, Dracula, a Briton, or a Scot. Phrases such as the following ones may be used:

   "What?"   "Hello. I haven't seen you in a long time."
   "Maybe."   "Brrr. I am freezing."

ACADEMIC VARIATIONS:

Parts of Speech: This activity can be used to review adjectives, adverbs, synonyms, antonyms, homonyms, and emotions. In reviewing adjectives, for example, the teacher says a word such as *mountain*. The students go around the circle and call out a word that describes a mountain.

Science or Social Studies: The teacher calls out a word pertaining to something the class has been studying such as *tropical rain forests*. The students, one at a time, name one thing that relates to that subject (e.g. *humidity, density, undergrowth, South America*).

Storytelling: Have your students use this activity to provide sound effects for stories as you read them.

FLOURISHES:

For older students (grades 4-6). Give each student a scarf. Ask a question such as, "Are you feeling all right?" The student sitting next to the teacher, using the scarf as a character prop (e.g., old lady's head scarf, bride's veil, robber's mask, skier's broken arm sling) must give a reply as the character might. For example, if the scarf is a robber's mask, "Yes, now give me all your money," or "No, but I will be when you hand over your jewels." Continue around the circle with students answering the question in character, then asking the same question of the student seated next to them.

Lotsa Balls

GRADE LEVEL: 1-6

MATERIALS: 12 or more assorted rubber balls, 2 containers for the balls

AREA: gym or classroom

TIME NEEDED: 15 minutes

PURPOSE: To reinforce concentration skills, to practice short term memory, to follow directions, to maintain continuity, to practice sequencing, to work together as a group, to show responsibility. This is a great visual metaphor for working together, for observing sequencing, and for accountability.

PROCEDURES:

1. Take the students to an open space such as the gym, cafeteria, or outside. Ask the class to stand in a circle. Place 12 or 13 rubber balls of varying sizes into a container and place the container by your feet.

2. Toss one ball to a student. That student will toss the ball to another student who will toss the ball to another student, and so on until every child has caught the ball. Stress to the students that they must remember who tossed them the ball and to whom they tossed it. That order will not change throughout this activity.

3. Place the empty container on the ground by the person who will catch the ball last. That person will put each ball into the container as it is caught.

4. Now the fun begins. Following the established order, begin tossing balls until all 12 or 13 are being tossed from one person to another. You may want to model ways to throw the ball so that they are catchable. Younger students may want to roll the ball on the ground or floor, while older students may find that an underhand toss is easier to control than an overhead throw. At any rate, it is important that the balls be tossed in such a manner as to be catchable. A student who drops a ball is responsible for retrieving it and tossing it to the appropriate person.

ACADEMIC VARIATIONS:

Reading: Have students sit on the floor in a circle. Ask one student to hold a ball and begin telling a story. After a few seconds, the student will stop talking and roll the ball to another student who must continue where the first student left off.

Reinforce the letters of the alphabet by tossing the balls to students and have them call out a word that begins with an "A" when they catch the first ball, a "B" when they catch the second ball, and so on.

Math: Sitting on the floor, three students will take turns rolling a ball to each other. three other students who are observing will try to duplicate the pattern.

FLOURISHES:

On a day when there have been a few problems on the playground, and some rules have been broken, bring the students back into the room for a bit of role-playing. Using scarves, wigs, or hats and water-soluble markers, convert the balls into hand puppets that can be used as characters for the role-playing. The students will let the rubber people do the talking to resolve the situation.

Mystery Movement

GRADE LEVEL: K-6

MATERIALS: none

AREA: open floor space

TIME NEEDED: 10 minutes

PURPOSE: To strengthen observation skills, to practice following directions, to develop patterning and rhythm skills.

PROCEDURES:

1. Direct students to sit in a circle on the floor.

2. Select someone to be "It," and ask that person to leave the room.

3. Select someone to be the "leader" and to begin making a rhythmic movement (e.g., clapping hands, thumping head, patting knees, snapping fingers, moving arms up and down, etc.). Everyone in the circle must imitate the leader. If the leader changes movements, everyone in the circle must change also. The leader can have everyone sitting or standing, as long as they remain in a circle.

4. The object is for "It" to come back to the center of the circle, watch the group, and try to guess who is initiating movement patterns.

   It is important that the movement leader change the movement patterns frequently, and that the rest of the students avoid looking directly at the leader, so they don't give "It" any clues about who the leader might be.

   Hint: Suggest to students that they look at the person directly across the circle from them. If everyone in the circle does this, it will be almost impossible for "It" to figure out who the leader is, because only one person is, in reality, looking at the leader.

5. "It" gets three chances to guess who the leader is. Once the leader has been "discovered," the leader gets to pick someone else to be "It." The new "It" will then leave the room. The former "It" gets to pick someone to be the new leader who begins a new rhythm pattern.

ACADEMIC VARIATIONS:

Use this activity to reinforce patterning skills in math, following directions, motor skills development, and the importance of having fun.

FLOURISHES:

Make this a *body* game. First the leader begins movement/rhythm patterns by using only facial movements (e.g., blinking eyes, twitching nose, sticking out tongue). A second participant uses only neck to waist movements (e.g., shoulder shrug, elbow touching) and so on down the body. At the end of the activity have the class sequence the movements once again from beginning to end or from end to beginning.

Pantomime Warm-ups

GRADE LEVEL: 2-6

MATERIALS: none

AREA: floor space

TIME NEEDED: 20 minutes

PURPOSE: To develop awareness of nonverbal communication, to enhance self-expression, to practice working together.

PROCEDURES:

Group Exercises

1. Ask the students to sit in a circle.

2. Ask the students to demonstrate, through body movement and facial expression (pantomime), the following actions, verbally first, then nonverbally:

waking up	swimming underwater
picking apples	bowling
chewing bubble gum	climbing a ladder
mowing a lawn	lifting a stack of boxes
painting a ceiling	drinking a glass of water

3. Now ask the students to get into groups and do the following things nonverbally first, then verbally:

put up a tent	pull a heavy boat
ring a heavy bell	build a sand castle
build a fire	lift a heavy box
extinguish a fire	play tug-of-war

Handing Off

1. Ask the students to stand in a circle.

2. Explain that one at a time, going around the circle, they will pretend to hand off the following objects to the person standing next to them:

a stack of dishes	a handful of mud
a bowling ball	an ice cube
a basket of eggs	a smelly rag
a hot potato	a cactus
a poisonous snake	a worm
a heavy brick	a stack of cardboard boxes

Facial Warm-ups

1. Ask the students to sit in a circle.

2. Direct the students to use only their faces to become:

happy	nervous
sad	relaxed
angry	anxious
surprised	tired
scared	dismayed
snobby	perplexed
bored	

3. Between each facial emotion, the students should show a neutral face. This can be done by making their face normal or by sliding their hand down over their face as if wiping the emotion away. Students can also lower their heads when finished with one emotion, then bring their faces up when beginning a new one.

Body Warm-ups

1. The class sits in a circle on the floor.

2. Direct the students to use their bodies to become:

full of air	a TV antenna
water	bicycle handlebars
a ball	wind
pudding	a pebble
the letter c	a balloon

Walking Warm-ups

1. Direct a few students at a time to stand at one end of the room.

2. Ask them to walk from one end of the room to the other in the following ways:

    normally
    without walking in front of or behind another person
    as quietly as they can
    as noisily as they can
    with eyes closed (monitor this one closely)
    in as straight a line as possible
    the shortest way they can imagine to get from one end of the room to the other; the longest,
       the strangest, the flattest, etc.
    on one foot
    using neither hands nor feet
    with a partner, using no feet and no hands
    with three people, using only two feet and two hands
    make up own mode of movement across the room

3. Ask the students to find their own space in the room and stand there.

4. Now ask the students to walk as if they were the following:

a pirate	an octopus
a teenager	a cowboy
an old person	a tightrope walker
a snake	in new shoes

Walk and Talk

1. Ask the students to find their own space in the room.

2. On the count of 10, students will use their bodies to create a being from outer space or an original animal (e.g., part elephant, part monkey). Then they will freeze.

3. On the count of 10 again, the students will begin to move like that alien creature or newly created animal. No sound, just movement.

4. On the count of 10 once more, the students will move like their creature or animal and make a sound that it might make.

5. Now on the final count of 10, the students will create a special manner in which to ask a question while in character of the other creatures or animals as they pass by them (e.g., "Could you tell me where the nearest restaurant is?").

FLOURISHES:

On a nice spring day, take the class outside, find a nice grassy spot on the playground, and lie back, looking at the different cloud shapes. When students see a cloud shape they can recognize let them stand up and pantomime the shape they have just seen. Others in the class must guess what the pantomime is and then try to find it in the sky. This is a great excuse to get outside and have a date with nature.

Scavenger Hunt

GRADE LEVEL: 1-6

MATERIALS: list of items on slips of paper

AREA: classroom and surrounding school environment

TIME NEEDED: 10 minutes

PURPOSE: To create an atmosphere of discovery, to recognize objects that begin with specific letters of the alphabet, to work in a group, to locate specific objects, to develop self-discipline, and gain a sense of completion.

PROCEDURES:

1. Appropriate to the age group and content area being studied, make a list of 10 objects that can be found in the classroom, around the school, or on the playground.

2. Divide the children into groups of three. Give each group a list.

3. Make sure a member of each group is wearing a watch that has been synchronized with the classroom wall clock.

4. Give the groups the exact time they are to return, whether they have found all of the objects or not. A time limit of six to eight minutes is plenty of time for most of the objects to be gathered. Some groups will be able to find all of the objects, some will not.

5. Explain to the groups that they will have eight minutes to either stay in the classroom or go outside to find as many of the objects on their list as possible. Remind them that they must be back in the classroom at the prearranged time, or their objects will not be counted.

6. Count to 10 and send them on their way. Be sure that everyone knows the boundaries of this exercise. Where can they go? What is out-of-bounds? Will someone be with them if they choose to go out to the playground?

7. When all of the groups have returned and displayed their objects, discuss the commonalities of the objects and where they were found. Tie in your reason for asking them to get those specific objects.

    For individual groups, here are some suggested objects that apply to specific content areas:

Math

Find five objects that are circles.
Find eight pieces of chalk of varying lengths. Measure the lengths.
Find 20 pennies.
Find the word "nine" on six different things.
Find five objects that are square.
Find 10 similar looking stones.
Find five leaves that have more than three points on each leaf.

Find five things that are in groups (e.g., grapes, flower petals).
Find four objects each of which have three parts.
Find eight small objects. Put them in order by weight.

Language Arts

Find 10 things that begin with the letter *s*.
Find 10 things that begin with the first 10 letters of the alphabet.
Find 10 things that are small.
Find 10 things that have the word "story" in them.
Find 10 books about 10 different animals.
Find 10 pictures of faces.
Find 10 words that are written differently and end in "-ing."
Find 10 ways to describe a tree.
Find 10 pictures of 10 different dogs.
Find 10 things that are round.

Science/Environment/Health

Find 10 things that pollute.
Find 10 things that are good for you.
Find 10 things that can be harmful to you.
Find 10 pictures, paragraphs, or books that have to do with space.
Find 10 pictures of weather.
Find 10 things that are the seven colors found in a prism, plus something black, something
    white, and something clear.
Find 10 things that make 10 different sounds.
Find 10 things that are fire hazards.
Find 10 different kinds of seeds.
Find five hard objects and five soft objects.

FLOURISHES:

Students will write down their first and last names. (In order to make this variation fair, be sure
that the number of letters used is consistent among all of the boys and girls. Some students may have
to use their middle names, and some may have to drop a few letters from their names.) Using the
letters that make up their names, the students will race to find objects that begin with those letters.
The first one back with all of the objects wins a trip to the bathroom without asking permission.

Scarves

GRADE LEVEL: K-6

MATERIALS: colorful, lightweight scarves

AREA: open floor space

TIME NEEDED: 10 minutes

PURPOSE: To develop coordination, to show spatial relationships, to practice movement, to follow directions, to enhance creative expression, to illustrate geometric or letter shapes.

PROCEDURES:

1. Give each student a scarf. (Scarves can be purchased inexpensively at local five-and-dime stores, discount stores, or thrift shops, and can also be found at garage sales. Polyester, chiffon, or light, woven fabrics work best.)

2. Explain to students that you want them to ball their scarf up and toss it into the air without catching it. Ask them to watch it float to the floor. What did it remind them of? A cloud? A leaf? A parachute?

3. Now ask the students to follow directions by tossing the scarves into the air and catching them in the following ways:

   with one hand, then the other.
   with one foot, then the other.
   on one shoulder, then the other.
   behind their backs.
   spinning in a circle, then catching it.
   with a partner, tossing the two scarves up together and catching the other person's scarf.
   be creative.

4. Show geometric shapes such as circles, squares, rectangles, triangles, and octagons on the chalkboard or on tagboard pieces, and have the students move their scarves in the air, making those shapes. Practice with each hand.

5. Have each student use a scarf as something other than a scarf (e.g., old woman's hat, bridal veil, parachute, karate belt, etc.). Allow the students time to describe the character that goes with the scarf prop and what the character might say or do.

ACADEMIC VARIATIONS:

Adverbs: Use the scarves to act out adverbs. For example, slowly, quickly, etc.

Science: Move the scarves to show cloud patterns or wind patterns.

Spelling: Practice spelling words in the air with the scarves.

Writing: Make cursive writing movements in the air or on the floor with the scarves.

FLOURISHES:

We have found scarves to be very useful in dance classes, when boys and girls get to the age where they don't even want to touch each other, much less hold hands. Give each child a scarf and let the class hold scarves instead of hands while dancing. Unless we're mistaken, cooties don't climb polyester.

Chapter 2

DRAMA

drama (drä ma) *n.* 1: a method of communication using characterization 2: what Arnold Schwarzenegger does for a living 3: a teaching method that brings reality and fantasy to your classroom 4: a solution to boredom 5: energy 6: reinforcement 7: fun.

Drama. Sounds heavy to me. Sounds heavy and difficult and time-consuming. Sounds like rehearsals and costumes and sets and stages and scripts, and it definitely sounds like too much work. Well, maybe not.

What is drama in the classroom? It can be rehearsals and costumes and sets and stages and scripts and props. But, it is also pantomime, puppetry, storytelling, role-playing, and poetry. And it is theater and choral reading. It is a variety of ways in which students creatively express themselves. It is life, communication, energy, and expansion. It is self-discovery. It is magic.

You are probably using drama in your classroom more than you realize. When you say, "Pretend you are...;" when you state, "Show me what you mean...;" and when you ask, "How would that person feel, act, or react?" you are using drama in your classroom. When you ask students to walk around the room like elephants, float like snowflakes, sit like rocks, or become shadows, you are using drama. When you ask students to "shed their skins" and crawl into someone else's, that is drama.

So, how do we prepare our classrooms to use drama? How do we make sure it doesn't become too much work, but, rather, an essential part of our classroom? We simply take the challenge, and create the environment. We give our students permission and more, encouragement, to "step out, step up, and step in." And we let it happen.

To ensure that the environment in your classroom is conducive to informal drama activities, here are a few "musts" for your classroom:

1. **Bag of costumes**. This could be old clothes, hats, shoes, gloves, army attire, old Halloween costumes, old sheet, and neckties. Buy these at secondhand stores, or go to garage sales at closing time. By then, people are so tired, they may give you the leftovers for free. In fact, they'll probably pay you just to move it off their front lawn. This is a great way to get neat old hats and neckties.

2. **Cassette tape recorder and tapes**. Collect sound effects tapes, soundtracks from movies and Broadway shows, electronic music, mood music, folk music, and song lyrics.

3. **Synthesizer or autoharp**.

4. **Percussion instruments**. Percussion instruments add flavor to storytelling, dramatic presentations, and movement activities. You'll want tambourines, Latin percussion instruments, bells, whistles, kazoos, sticks, cymbals, and shakers. Make them yourself, or buy them one at a time at your local band store or from companies we have listed in the appendix on page 209.

5. **Puppets**. There are all kinds: paper plate, paper sack, box, string, cylinder, rod, tin can, finger, sock, Styrofoam cup, milk carton, shadow, balloon, Styrofoam ball, hot pad, gloves, even ready-made ones.

6. **A bag of "smells."** You can use any object with a distinct aroma: pine cones, potpourri, cinnamon sticks, rubber, and perfumes, for example.

7. **Media collection**. This is a collection of unusual poems, stories, newspaper articles, magazine pictures, 35mm slides, and black and white prints.

8. **A video camera and videocassette**. Don't be afraid to let those little short folks use it. What good is a camera that is safely tucked away in the AV room?

9. **A 35mm camera with film**. Black and white prints are interesting to use.

10. **A box of makeup**. Students can bring leftover makeup from home to start a classroom stage makeup box. Be selective, though.

11. **Clown white**. Wait until Halloween is over, then hit the overstock sales.

12. **Fabric collection**. This could be scarves, old sheets, material scraps, ribbon, and so on.

13. **A box of props**. Rubber noses, eyeglass frames, gloves, old jewelry, walking canes, wigs, hairpieces, and masks are ideal.

14. **Cardboard boxes**. Think of all the possibilities: a dragon's cave, a troll's hideout, a spaceship, a newscaster's desk.

15. **Storage space**. If you're lucky, the room across the hall from yours will be empty. You'll need it.

When attempting any form of creative dramatics in the elementary classroom, there are certain aspects that should be given some thought. *Projection* is one. Those short people in your room (or even the big short people in the intermediate grades) are not used to formal or informal public speaking. For the most part, when they're in front of the class, they have trouble speaking at all. We call it "Intimidation Factor Number One." Mumbling is common, and mumbling with one's head directed toward the stained carpet or chipped tile flooring is even more the norm. Letting the students find their comfort zones is the key here. These wee folk need to feel comfortable, secure, and above all, in control of the situation.

When students begin to feel comfortable just standing up in front of the class, or standing up, period, then you can work on projection, and that takes nothing but practice, practice, practice. Give the students a line to say, or a poem to read, or a word definition to repeat. Ask them to say it normally, then again and again as you work your way toward the back of the room. Do it gradually, methodically, often. Describe the difference between speaking loudly with control and screaming. They will know the difference. The veins in your neck will tell them.

Once you hear your students, it is time to introduce a new word, *voicelife*, which is the art of using emotion, nuance, and liveliness in your voice. It is a way of making your voice sound colorful, understandable, and authentic. Then ask, Is the way the students are speaking interesting to the ear? Do the words sound full? Are they clear? Do their voices fluctuate? Do they soften? Do they broaden, or do they sound colorless and flat? Performers seem to have voicelife naturally (but only after years of hard work). Many teachers have developed the skill. But the little guys and gals in class have to be taught and the best way to teach them is by (and you may not be ready for this) modeling. You do it, then they do it. You speak with expression, then they speak with expression. You yell with anger, then they yell with anger. You speak with sadness, then they speak with sadness.

Now on with the show.

Act It/Draw It

GRADE LEVEL: 3-6

MATERIALS: index cards with word on each card
desktop bell
newsprint or drawing paper
markers or crayons

AREA: large open space

TIME NEEDED: 20 minutes

PURPOSE: To strengthen coordination, to enhance listening skills, to demonstrate creative expression, to practice thinking quickly, and to work in a group situation.

PROCEDURES:

1. Divide the class into four even groups. Designate groups as A, B, C, D. The groups will compete against each other.

2. Place a table or desk at each corner of the room. Place several markers and a stack of newsprint, drawing paper, or scratch paper on each table.

3. Put another desk or stool in the center of the activity area. On top of that desk or stool place a desktop bell or similar object that makes a sound.

4. Have each group count off. The students who are #1 will be the first to draw. Those students will stand in front of each table with marker in hand. The other group members will stand behind each table. The teacher will stand behind the stool with the bell on it. Tell the students that those who are drawing cannot communicate verbally or with their body in any way.

5. When everyone is ready, all the drawers will stand by the teacher where they will be shown a card with a word on it. When teacher says, "Go," the drawers will race to their respective tables and begin drawing a picture of the word. As they draw, other members of their group will begin calling out what they think the drawing is.

6. Once the correct word is heard, the student doing the drawing races to the center, rings the bell, and calls out the correct response. Whoever rings the bell first and has the right answer gets a point for the team.

7. Students who are #2 are now ready to do the same thing, and so on and so on.

8. As a change of pace, the teacher can opt to have the participants act out the word instead of drawing it. The same rules apply.

ACADEMIC VARIATIONS:

Vocabulary Words and Spelling Words: This is a creative way to review the meanings of vocabulary words.

Science: Allow students to play this game as a concept review for science topics. It works especially well with areas like simple machines, weather, the human body, health, and plants.

Social Studies: Use this activity to review the major ideas and vocabulary for your unit. If the unit was the Westward Movement: wagon, Oregon trail, stamped, branding, cowboys, barbed wire, etc.

Math: Use flash cards with math problems (12-7 =). Students who are acting or drawing either draw a picture problem (no numbers) or act out a math story whose problem is 12-7 = .

Reading: Similar to the game "Charades," students will act out or draw titles of their favorite books.

FLOURISHES:

This one is great for honing the sense of sound. Give each team member a blindfold. This time, the active participant goes to the teacher who is holding cards which have phrases written on them instead of words (e.g., The Gettysburg Address, an elephant stampede, center ring at a circus, a bunch of bees stinging, etc.).

Team members put on the blindfolds and listen as the active participant comes back to the group and verbally gives only appropriate sounds as clues to the phrase. For example, if the answer is a bunch of bees stinging, the actor will run around, screaming and yell "Get off of me!" or "Water, water, I need to jump in that pond." It is very important that all students refrain from using words that would be dead giveaways (e.g., bees, hive, sting, etc.). With this particular variation, it is important that the exact phrase be given as the answer.

Begin It

GRADE LEVEL: 4-6

MATERIALS: chairs
boxes
stools
scarves
gloves
prop box

AREA: classroom

TIME NEEDED: 30+ minutes

PURPOSE: To promote creative thinking and expression through a drama format; to predict a logical conclusion of an idea; to review sequencing; and to create a story structure (beginning, middle, and end).

PROCEDURES:

1. Divide the boys and girls into groups of four or five students.

2. Give each group a slip of paper with one of the following sentences written on it:

    "Gosh, it's spooky in here."
    "I don't know how I let you talk me into this."
    "What is that on the floor?"
    "So, you must be the new baby-sitter."
    "What's that on your nose?"
    "Yikes!"
    "Did you hear that noise?"
    "Will someone see who's at the door?"
    "Those are the biggest footprints I have ever seen."
    "Look! A cave!"
    "Whew, it's dark in here."
    "Pardon me, but I can't help noticing that you have green hair."
    "What is that under the bridge?"
    "I love going on picnics."
    "I've never been on a horse before."

3. Direct each group to create a short skit in which the first words spoken must be the sentence that is written on the slip of paper.

4. Remind students that the skit should make sense, and the sequence of it should be logical and clearly understood. Allow approximately five to six minutes to develop the skit, depending on the age group.

ACADEMIC VARIATIONS:

Social Studies: Skits can be a review of current events, class rules, vocabulary words, specific historic occurrences, geographical locations.

Reading: This activity can be used to create original fairy tales or fables, or review the meaning of idioms. For example, "I really lost my head."

Science: Skits can provide an interesting review of scientific concepts such as characteristics of different planets, systems of the body, mammals, the cyclical nature of life, and the lives of famous people of science.

Math: Skits are a fun way to practice writing, solving, and reflecting on story problems.

Health: Give each group the same beginning sentence ("Have you ever used drugs?") and allow each group to create a skit that answers that question. Comparing skits, and the manner in which each group answered that question, would make for an interesting discussion. This is a great way to lead into the DARE (drug abuse resistance education) program, or a drug-awareness unit.

FLOURISHES:

Allow students to use the scarves during the Begin It or End It activities to define their characters, as props for the skit, or for any other use they can come up with.

Conversation Freeze

GRADE LEVEL: 5-6

MATERIALS: bell or percussion instrument for giving signal

AREA: classroom

TIME NEEDED: 20 minutes

PURPOSE: To strengthen communication skills, to develop character definition, to stress continuity, to practice listening skills, to enhance conversational skills.

PROCEDURES:

1. Two students (#1 and #2) stand in front of the classroom and begin having an improvisational conversation, using normal conversational gestures as they speak (talking with hands, scratching their heads, yawning, etc.).

2. At a hand clap by the teacher, both students will immediately freeze their words and actions.

3. Another student, #3, will go to the front of the classroom and take the place of student #1, making sure to take the exact stance and position as student #1.

4. Student #3 will then begin a new conversation with student #2, one that relates in some way to the shape that the body is in. Student #2 will pick up the conversation and they will continue that conversation until another hand clap is sounded. Both freeze.

5. At that signal, another student will come forward and take the place of student #2, imitating exactly that student's stance. The new student will then begin a new conversation that relates to the position of student #3, and the cycle continues.

6. This exercise should continue until everyone in the class has had a chance to be a part of a conversation.

ACADEMIC VARIATIONS:

Social Studies: The teacher calls out a time in history, such as the Revolutionary War. The two students must then become two characters from that time period and converse accordingly. (For example, a Redcoat and a patriotic silversmith.) When the teacher claps, the new person becomes a different character from that time period and begins a new conversation.

Geography: Two characters represent, through conversation, the different viewpoints of their region of the world or country.

Current Events: The characters interact with various viewpoints about a current event, their stance or body shape determines their attitude.

Science: Two students begin discussing the circulation or digestive system. At a signal, they freeze. Another student comes up, takes the place of student #1 and continues the discussion where that student left off. For this activity to work smoothly, the students must know the appropriate material. This is an excellent means of reviewing for a test, plus the review material is presented in a different way, making it a bit more interesting.

Reading: The students become characters from a given story. Their body stances and shapes determine what conversation will occur.

FLOURISHES:

Give students a hat to wear before this activity begins. With the use of hats, the characters are defined to some extent. The conversation can go in any direction, but the flavor of the conversation must be in tune with the character that the hat represents.

To make it even more difficult, toss a hat to the students just as they are about to begin a new conversation. This will really require your students to think on their feet.

Emotion Melody

GRADE LEVEL: 3-6

MATERIALS: none

AREA: classroom

TIME NEEDED: 15 minutes

PURPOSE: To introduce or review human emotions through movement and sound skills; to strengthen teamwork skills.

PROCEDURES:

1. Lead a discussion on emotions and why we feel them. Remind students that there are many kinds of emotions other than sad, mad, and glad. It is also helpful to list some emotions on the board and ask the students when these emotions might be felt, or in what situations they might occur.

   Some different emotions might be: boredom, snobbishness, anxiety, impatience, shyness, disgust, surprise, yearning, agitation, excitement, numbness, bewilderment, aloofness, regret, ecstasy, sympathy, delight, incredulity, peacefulness, craziness, enthusiasm, meanness, sleepiness, aggravation.

2. Divide students into pairs.

3. Each pair will select an emotion. They will decide on a sound and a movement to go with that particular emotion.

   If the emotion was surprise, the sound could be "Yikes!" and the movement might be bringing your hands to your face in a wide gesture.

4. Give student pairs time to practice their emotion, then ask all the pairs to stand in a horseshoe configuration facing the teacher or leader who now will become the "Emotion Conductor."

5. The object is for each emotion to become a musical instrument as in a symphony orchestra and for each pair of students to act out their emotion when the Emotion Conductor points to them. Pairs continue playing the emotion over and over until the Conductor cuts them off.

ACADEMIC VARIATIONS:

The same format can be used when studying or reviewing:

Animals: animal sounds/movements.

Vocabulary Words: word/meaning.

Nouns: word/sound.

Blends: movement/sound.

Review of States or State Capitals: Each pair thinks of a state and its capital. The name of the capital city must be said and a movement must be done in a way that describes the particular state. For example, if the city is Austin, Texas, the word *Austin* might be said with a Texas accent and the movement might be roping a calf or standing bowlegged with thumbs in pants pockets.

Geographic Regions: Use this activity to describe an area of the country or a tourist attraction or product.

FLOURISHES:

Cut out letters of the alphabet (the more the better). Allow each pair of students to randomly select six or so letters without looking. Pairs then try to make up a nonsense word using only the letters they have selected (e.g., "glxopp"), and an appropriate movement to go with it.

You might want to go even further and have kids write a story about their new word ("There once was a glxopp who lived deep in the ocean..."), or make up sentences that they think would fit with their new word ("When Mother spread the glxopp on the floor, our pet dog kept getting its paws stuck in it").

End It

GRADE LEVEL: 4-6

MATERIALS: scarves
boxes
wigs
masks
prop box
folding chairs

AREA: classroom

TIME NEEDED: 30+ minutes

PURPOSE: To predict a meaningful, logical, conclusion; to creatively express ideas through a structured drama format; to practice cooperative learning; to review sequencing; to create a story structure (beginning, middle, and end).

PROCEDURES:

1. Divide the class into groups of four or five students.

2. Give each group a slip of paper with one of the following sentences written on it:

   "And that's why no one goes into that house anymore."
   "So, that's what happened to the treasure map."
   "Well, I've learned my lesson the hard way."
   "Run!"
   "You mean he ate the whole thing?"
   "And the rabbit and the squirrel lived happily ever after."
   "I guess we were all pretty brave."
   "I've never been so scared in my whole life."
   "Thank you, Mr. President. I'll keep it always."
   "It goes to show you, four brains are better than one."
   "I never knew I could climb that high."
   "And that is why the sun is yellow."
   "Who knew how long the ship had been sunk."
   "And the two-headed calf was never seen again."
   "The magic pod suddenly exploded and sent millions of crystals all over the meadow."

3. Direct each group to create a short skit in which the concluding sentence of the skit is the one written on the slip of paper. Allow approximately five to six minutes to develop the skit, depending on the age group.

4. Remind students that the skit should make sense and the ending should be logical and clearly understood.

ACADEMIC VARIATIONS:

Punctuation Marks: The last sentence must end with a certain punctuation mark. For example, He really did it! He really did it? He really did it.

Social Studies: The last sentence could relate to a holiday, specific event in history, foreign phrase, adage, or current event. The skit could reflect real facts relating to the topic being studied.

Reading: The last sentence could end with a moral from an Aesop's Fable, or an ending to a well-known fairy tale. This activity could also be a review of vocabulary words and definitions.

FLOURISHES:

Give the students hats or neckties to use as props, or to define their characters. A hint for keeping hats clean and to maintain health codes: Have students wear thin shower caps, like those you can get at motels, when using hats.

Freeze Frame

GRADE LEVEL: 4-6

MATERIALS: none

AREA: classroom

TIME NEEDED: 25 minutes

PURPOSE: To strengthen problem solving skills, to practice cooperative learning, to develop listening skills, to review academic concepts, to understand sequencing.

PROCEDURES:

1. Divide the children into groups of five. Allow students time to think of something they have been studying in social studies or science. For example, community helpers.

2. The group will select one community helper and discuss all of the different characters that relate to that particular community helper. If the community helper is a dentist, the related characters might be: patient, dental assistant, parent, and office secretary.

3. The group will then decide on one scene in which each student can play a character that has been discussed. They will also think of appropriate dialogue to go with that scene.

4. After some practice time, each group will go to the front of the class and begin by freezing their characters in an appropriate scene. For example: the patient will be lying back in a chair; the dentist will be examining his teeth; the dental assistant will be holding a suction cup; the parent will be sitting near the patient; and the office secretary will be standing away from the dentist with a telephone held to her ear.

5. As soon as the group is frozen into position, other class members will try to guess what the scenario is, who the characters are, and what the characters are doing. The group remains frozen until the class has guessed. Then, the group will bring their characters to life through appropriate dialogue. "Doctor, it's my back tooth that really hurts." "Yes, son, way in the back. Looks like the beginning of a cavity to me." "Do you need me to suction it, Doctor?" "Doctor, there's a call for you on line 4." "Honey, have you been brushing like I told you to?"

ACADEMIC VARIATIONS: Any content area.

FLOURISHES:

During National Book Week, you can show off how smart your kids are. Divide your students into groups and let each group select a favorite book. The scenario they freeze into will be the book title. This one is tricky, so they will really need to think about this. Invite another class to come in and try to guess what the book titles are. When the guessing is over, let your kids teach the kids in the other class how to do this activity, and let the other class have a go at it. Better yet, have mixed groups.

Grandstand

GRADE LEVEL: 3-6

MATERIALS: 4 chairs

AREA: classroom

TIME NEEDED: 20 minutes

PURPOSE: To work cooperatively, to communicate nonverbally, to change a nonverbal situation to a verbal interaction, to practice sequencing skills.

PROCEDURES:

1. Place four chairs side by side in front of the room.

2. Divide the class into groups of four students.

3. Each group decides on a situation wherein they are watching or are spectators at some event. Teachers working with younger students may want to select the event.

4. After three or four minutes of practice time, each group goes to the front of the class, and sits in the chairs, pretending to watch an event such as a baseball game, a tennis match, or a rodeo. The rest of the class must guess what event the spectators are watching based on their movements and facial expressions. This activity should be done nonverbally at first. If the class cannot guess, the group begins again, this time adding words that go with particular actions.

   Suggested events are:

football game	car race	watching TV
rock concert	basketball game	bull fight
Miss America Pageant	pie eating contest	bungee jumping
skydiving exhibition	scary movie	tennis match
boxing match	sad movie	fireworks

ACADEMIC VARIATIONS:

   Social Studies: Each group selects a time in history, or a specific event during the period they are studying, and watch something that might have occurred during that time. For example, the building of the pyramids, Washington crossing the Delaware, or the Boston Tea Party.

   Geography: A group can pretend to be on vacation somewhere in the geographic area of the United States, watching some event or activity unique to that area. For example, Old Faithful at Yellowstone or volcanic action in Hawaii.

FLOURISHES:

   Give each person in the group a hat. With the hats as a definition of their character, the group members must think of an event at which they are spectators. They should watch the event as their characters would. For example, at a football game, a little old lady, a farmer, a construction worker, and a teenager might all react differently to what they are seeing. As an alternative, have the players think of a certain character and speak and act like that character, but wear another kind of hat. The class must connect the hats with the correct characters after the skit. This one takes a lot of thinking.

Human Machines

GRADE LEVEL: 4-6

MATERIALS: none

AREA: classroom

TIME NEEDED: 30 minutes

PURPOSE: To strengthen cooperative learning abilities, to practice logical sequencing, to express ideas through creative movement.

PROCEDURES:

1. Divide the class into groups of five or more.

2. Lead a brief discussion on machines and how they work. Stress that many machines are made up of smaller parts that, when working together, produce a common product or end result.

3. Ask students to think of machine-like movements and machine-like sounds to go with those movements.

4. Have four volunteers come to the front of the class. Explain that they will be making a hot dog machine. Ask the first person to act out a sound and movement for the first part of the machine. While the first person continues, the second person in the group will come forward, connect in some logical way with the first person, and begin a sound and movement that makes sense as the second part of the machine. This continues until all group members have joined the machine.

5. Once the students understand the process, give each group the name of a machine to create. Provide ample time for each group to practice (approximately five to eight minutes), reminding them that each machine component should make logical sense for that particular machine.

6. Some fun machines to create include:

bubble gum blower	ice cube maker
pizza maker	taffy puller
soda pop machine	milk shake maker
copy machine	car washing machine
pencil sharpener	record player
gumball machine	doughnut making machine
washing machine	helium balloon pump

7. When all groups are ready, let each group show their machine to the rest of the class who will try to guess what kind of machine it is.

ACADEMIC VARIATIONS:

Science: In a unit on simple machines, the students can use their bodies to demonstrate how different machines like levers, pulleys, or inclined planes work, and to devise new ways to use simple machines in the creation of more complex machines. When studying the systems of the body, the Human Machines activity can be varied such that the students create machines that demonstrate the functions of those systems. In a study of space, this activity can be adapted to create machines that would function in a given space environment or be helpful to space travelers.

Social Studies: Dealing with current events related to technology or environmental issues, the students can create human machines that would help to solve or remedy a given problem, such as a machine to clean up an oil slick or machines that will revolutionize transportation.

When studying different eras in history, have the students create a machine that was either actually used then or a new machine that would have been helpful for the people of that time to have. For example, helpful machines for the Anasazi Indians might have included a corn planter, an irrigation machine, or a machine to start fires. Another motivational variation is the invention of human time machines which transport the students to another time period either past or future.

Math: Students may become a large clock with a second hand, minute hand, and hour hand to practice telling time. When working with story problems, the class can become a human machine which acts out story problems or math facts. If the math equation is 4-2 = 2, a group might create a machine which will illustrate the problem. Four students enter the machine, which whirls, twirls, grinds, and spews out only two of the four students.

Phonics: Create any kind of machine. The sounds of the different parts must begin with a consonant blend (e.g., the sounds of *cl, pl, bl, fl*) or digraph (*ch*), sound like a short or long vowel, or be a word used in spelling or vocabulary study. If studying root words, prefixs, and suffixes, the machine parts will include the building of a word. The first machine part provides a prefix, the middle the root word, and the final part the suffix (e.g., mis-understand-ing). The same format will work with syllabication (e.g., mis-un-der-stand-ing).

Writing: The Human Machine activity can help illustrate the idea of a beginning, middle, and end to a sentence, paragraph, or story.

Reading: Assist storybook characters by creating a human machine that would aid them in their predicament. For example, in the Mother Goose nursery rhymes, what machine could help Humpty Dumpty get off the wall safely or get put back together again? This can lead into discussions about how the story would be different if the character had had access to the machine. From here, creative writing is a natural next step.

FLOURISHES:

Select three or four students to come to the front of the room, stand side by side, and create weird machine sounds and movements. Introduce this new machine as the first ever "Super Duper Change Computer."

Explain to the students that if they go into the machine at one end, when they come out at the other end, they will be the opposite of what they were when they entered. Demonstrate by entering the machine looking very sad. Walk behind the students who make up the machine. When you come out of the other side, be very happy. Now give each student a chance to go into the Super Duper Change Computer. Remind them to show or tell how they are going into the machine. Then the class will watch the change which occurs as they come out the other end.

If you happen to have an old empty refrigerator box lying around as teachers so often do let that be the Super Duper Change Computer. Allow the kids to decorate the box in a far out machine motif. The possibilities are endless. The box can also double as a puppet house, time-out spot, or a secluded reading hideaway.

Inanimate Objects

GRADE LEVEL: 4-6

MATERIALS: none

AREA: classroom

TIME NEEDED: 15 minutes

PURPOSE: To stimulate the imagination, to develop and refine speech skills, to combine the characteristics of animate objects and inanimate objects, to provide the opportunity to think from different perspectives.

PROCEDURES:

1. Direct students to find an appropriate place in the room that will become their own space for this activity.

2. Ask them to become an object they see in the classroom, then freeze in that position.

3. Ask students to think of what that object might say if it could talk. For example, a ruler might say, "If I have to measure one more thing, I am going to scream," or "Would someone get me out of this dark, dirty desk?" Allow students to give different answers.

4. Call out the following categories and ask students to be specific as they become an object and think of a sentence that those objects might say:

   something found in a dishwasher
   something found at a movie theater
   something found in a grocery cart
   something found in a school lunch box
   something found in your desk
   a type of road sign
   something found at a birthday party
   something found in a wallet
   something found in a furniture store
   something found in the trunk of a car
   something found in a baby's room

ACADEMIC VARIATIONS:

Vocabulary Words or Spelling Words: Use spelling and vocabulary words as the inanimate objects.

Parts of Speech: Have the students become something that is a noun or a verb. They will then use adjectives or adverbs correctly in describing themselves.

Descriptive Writing Skills: This is a fun way to begin a fictional creative writing assignment. It stimulates imaginative thinking.

Social Studies: Become an inanimate object found in a covered wagon going west. Say something that the object might say. Ask students what the object is and three things about that object that you have studied during the unit on the Old West.

Science: Use terminology and inanimate objects from the unit you are studying. The statement the object makes must include one fact about the object itself and one logical imaginary statement the object might make if it could talk. A piece of a coral reef might say, "I am found in shallow water and many creatures call me home. But I wish somebody would give me a box of Band-Aids, so I could help the divers I accidentally cut."

FLOURISHES:

After completing this activity, give each student an inanimate object to write about as a main character of a story, with humans taking on secondary roles in the plot. Another idea is to let students decide on a first person story about an inanimate object. Have students tell the story from the object's point of view without saying what it is. For example, a broom might say, "I usually start the morning standing on my head in the closet. I spend a lot of time upside down. When I am called upon to 'do my thing,' I go back and forth, back and forth, because that is the motion I find most comfortable. The lady of the house depends on me after a party, or when people are messy in the kitchen." Once the story is over, allow other students to guess what the inanimate object is.

Opposites

GRADE LEVEL: 2-6

MATERIALS: none

AREA: classroom

TIME NEEDED: 10 minutes

PURPOSE: To review antonyms and homonyms through body movement and sound.

PROCEDURES:

1. Ask students to select partners.

2. Have partners number themselves #1 or #2.

3. The teacher will call out a word. Student #1 will act out that word while student #2 acts out the opposite meaning of the word at the same time.

4. After several words have been called out, allow students to switch roles so that each partner has the chance to act out, not only the meaning, but the opposite meaning as well.

    Some suggested antonyms are:

happy/sad	smooth/rough	straight/crooked
neat/sloppy	brave/fearful	fast/slow
wet/dry	hungry/full	thick/thin
up/down	dirty/clean	strong/weak
sleepy/awake	dark/light	loud/soft
good/bad	rich/poor	high/low
hot/cold	hard/soft	neat/messy
big/small	sick/healthy	full/empty
nervous/calm		

    Some suggested homonyms are:

I/eye	pair/pear	blue/blew
son/sun	right/write	here/hear
tail/tale	real/reel	won/one
night/knight	vein/vane	tow/toe
read/red	flue/flew	made/maid

FLOURISHES:

Create an interactive bulletin board. Let the students draw, cut from magazines, or otherwise create pictures representing each of the opposites. Post half of the opposites on the bulletin board with hooks or envelopes, so the students can attach the matching opposite to the correct picture.

Paint and Powder

GRADE LEVEL: 4-6

MATERIALS: liquid makeup
compact makeup
powder
rouge or blush
lipstick
eyebrow pencils
cold cream
talcum powder
facial tissue
cotton balls
clown white
eye shadow
Halloween makeup of any kind
hand mirrors

AREA: classroom

TIME NEEDED: 45 minutes - 1 hour

PURPOSE: To enhance creative imagination, to visually define different characters, to practice makeup and costuming techniques.

PROCEDURES:

1. This activity requires some discussion of appropriate behavior. Students who involve themselves in this particular activity should have had some experience in skit work, role-playing, and discipline. In other words, don't try this one unless you have a fairly organized group of kids who can control themselves and follow directions well.

2. The students are paired off and given a supply of makeup, wigs, scarves, costumes, hats, etc. To save confusion, it is a wise idea to have supplies distributed evenly. Taking turns, they are to apply makeup to each other, creating a character of some kind. Once the makeup is applied, the partners add wigs, hats, costumes, and anything that is appropriate to the enhancement and definition of that character. Be sure to turn the video camera on for the makeup application portion of this activity. This kind of visual critique or reinforcement will show clearly what worked and what didn't. Plus the students love watching themselves as a new character emerges.

3. When makeup and costuming is complete, the students will look at themselves, add any final touches, and discuss their new characters.

4. Students will present a short verbal skit based upon these new characters. At the conclusion of the partner skits, several students can combine forces and create another skit with more than two characters.

ACADEMIC VARIATIONS:

Social Studies: Give each pair of students two famous figures from history. Once appropriate makeup and costuming has occurred, ask the pair to present a short dialogue between the two characters.

Health: In studying drug abuse or bicycle safety, for example, students may want to use makeup and costumes to define certain characters appropriate to the topic (e.g., parent, teacher, police officer, drug dealer, peer, sibling). Then four or five students can assume these roles, and participate in a panel discussion presenting the viewpoint their characters might take.

Reading: The students create a favorite character out of a book or novel and act and react to situations as that character might.

FLOURISHES:

Here are five surefire ways to get more makeup than you'll ever need. Be very careful when using old makeup, however. You may want to clean it up a bit before distributing it to your students. Old makeup that has never been used is, of course, the best.

1. Write a note home to the moms in the class asking them to clean out their purses and bathroom cabinets of all old or partially used makeup.

2. Write a note to Grandma or an aunt asking for any old wigs lying around the house, in the attic, or on their heads.

3. Put a request for makeup, wigs, hats, and old clothes in the school newsletter.

4. Put a want ad in the local paper. "Local 5th grade class in desperate need of old wigs, ties, clothes, hats, and costuming accessories for school project." (You might not want to ask for old makeup this way.)

5. Go to the local department store makeup counter. Tell them your story and ask for any makeup that may be going out of stock. Once again, the best time to buy makeup, costumes, wigs, masks, and other costuming supplies is after a holiday, such as Halloween. Items are usually marked down considerably.

Sequencing

GRADE LEVEL: 1-6

MATERIALS: none

AREA: classroom

TIME NEEDED: 15 minutes

PURPOSE: To reinforce sequencing skills, to improve cooperative learning skills.

PROCEDURES:

1. Think of scenarios that are familiar to the children. Divide each scenario into sequential order. Suggested scenarios are:

open cabinet	carry bucket
open peanut butter jar	pick berries
spread peanut butter on bread	see bumblebee
eat it	get stung
pay money	wake up
get ticket	brush teeth
buy popcorn	get dressed
see movie	eat breakfast
open door	go into store
sit	find candy
fasten seat belt	pay for it
start engine	eat candy

2. Write phrases for each scenario on a slip of paper and place them in a hat.

3. Divide the students into groups of four. Each student in a group will draw a slip of paper from the hat for that group's scenario.

4. Without giving the individuals in each group time to connect with each other, ask the groups, one at a time, to come to the front of the room and act out their scenarios in the correct order. This forces the students to decide individually when their particular part of the sequence might logically occur. If working with younger children, it is probably best to allow time for them to discuss the sequence.

ACADEMIC VARIATIONS:

Social Studies: Give each group a scenario in history such as the landing of the *Mayflower*, Paul Revere's ride, or Lewis and Clark meeting Sacajawea, and allow students to put them in sequential order. This also works well with current events.

Fire Drills: Have students review the correct steps to take during a fire drill.

Health: Students will sequence steps in the respiratory, circulatory, and other body systems. This sequencing activity also works well with first aid instruction.

Math: Have students put the steps in long division, multidigit multiplication, and story problems in sequential order.

FLOURISHES:

Divide students into groups of five or six and have them number off. Each group writes a story whose topic has been selected by the teacher. Each individual in the group, one at a time, writes a paragraph that sequences correctly with the paragraph before it. When all of the paragraphs have been written, the story will be complete.

Telephones

GRADE LEVEL: 3-6

MATERIALS: 2 telephones, 2 chairs, 2 tables

AREA: classroom

TIME NEEDED: 30 minutes

PURPOSE: To practice conversational skills, to practice communication skills, to review facts, to develop public speaking skills, to practice listening skills.

PROCEDURES:

1. Place two tables 10 feet apart. Place one telephone on each table. If there is wiring still attached to the telephones, connect them by splicing together the appropriate wires (your custodian will have this knowledge), and students will be able to hear each other through the telephone.

2. Direct a student to sit at each table. Ask these students to pick up their telephones, make a call to the other person, and begin a conversation with that person.

3. Here are some suggested conversation topics:

   • Two people assume the role of people from different cultures. One asks questions about the other's culture, the other uses what has been learned in class to answer the questions.

   • One person describes himself over the telephone, the other tries to guess who he is. For example, "I wear a red and blue costume, I really love telephone booths, and I work for a large newspaper company. Sometimes I can't see very well." The answer is Superman. Or, "Yes, I have lived in India most of my life. I am rather old now, and don't get around as well as I used to, although I still travel all over the world. I won the Nobel Prize. I guess my career would be helping people and healing the sick." The answer is Mother Teresa.

4. Give two students a situation and have them discuss how to solve the problem. For example, "A kid is continually beating up somebody on the playground. What would you do about it?"

ACADEMIC VARIATIONS:

Social Studies: Select two characters from the same or different periods in history and let them have a conversation regarding a national problem. For example, overpopulation, acid rain, or the homeless.

Inanimate Objects: Two students pretend to be inanimate objects. For example, a teeter-totter and a basketball. The two students will then have a conversation about playground rules and how students treat them.

Reading: Let the students assume the identities of characters in the books they are reading. Pretending to call another character, they will carry on a conversation about what happened to them that day in their book.

Science: Have a conference call with several different types of animals discussing their habitats and environmental concerns related to them. This could include extinct animals as well as domesticated ones.

FLOURISHES:

At the end of the school year let the students spend one afternoon having conversations with famous persons from history. Ask each student to think of one historical figure the class has studied during that school term. Give each student time to put together terms and traits that might describe this particular individual. Now allow the students one at a time to go to the telephone and "call" the rest of the class. The callers must describe who they are without using the figure's name, what their claim to fame is, where and when they lived, and so on. The information should be given in such a way as to make guessing challenging for the class. This is a great way to review or wrap up what you covered during the school year.

The Three Ws
(Who, What, Where)

GRADE LEVEL: 5-6

MATERIALS: list of *Who, What, Where* words (see page 42)

AREA: classroom

TIME NEEDED: 45 minutes

PURPOSE: To reinforce the idea of characterization, to develop creative writing skills, to promote self-expression, to demonstrate communication skills, to use imagination, to practice problem solving.

PROCEDURES:

1. Compile a list of *Who* words, a list of *What* phrases, and a list of *Where* phrases. Suggested lists of words are provided at the end of this activity.

2. Place all of the *Who* words into a hat or container, all of the *What* phrases into another hat, and all of the *Where* phrases into still another hat.

3. Divide the students into groups of five or more, and have each group pick one *Where* phrase and one *What* phrase. Now ask each member of the group to select one *Who* word.

4. Each group must now use the different *Whos*, the one *What* and the one *Where* they have selected to create a short skit depicting those three *Ws*. For example, Rambo, the President, a cowboy, an alien, and a clown, sunbathing at the North Pole.

5. These skits should be done verbally, as the different *Who* characters must use speech to help define their characters clearly.

6. Give reasonable time for rehearsal. After each presentation, other class members should be given a chance to guess the *Who, What,* and *Where* of the skit.

ACADEMIC VARIATIONS:

Social Studies: Ask students to put characters of different eras together to solve a universal problem. For example, Miles Standish, Napoleon, Columbus, and an astronaut on the Amazon River discussing deforestation.

Interpersonal Skills: Create a role-playing situation in which students work through classroom, playground, or personal problems such as fighting, bullying, disruptive behavior, or stealing.

Reading: Use book settings for the *Where*, characters from different stories the children are reading for the *Who*, and unusual plots for the *What*.

FLOURISHES:

Give each group a section of newspaper. Randomly, they must choose one *What* from an article, one *Where* from another article, and as many *Whos* from different articles as there are people in the group. Give each group ample time to create a logical skit that combines all of these *Ws*. When each skit is finished, ask the rest of the class why each group came up with the ending that it did. This is a good catalyst for debating issues.

Who List

Tarzan	forest ranger	ship captain	pilot
waitress	Homecoming Queen	deep sea diver	bull rider
old lady	President of the	policeman	train engineer
bronco rider	United States	Mickey Mouse	Sleeping Beauty
nun	wrestler	mountain climber	tennis player
shoplifting kid	Marilyn Monroe	magician	nurse
spy	bullfighter	cave man	football player
Little Miss Muffet	car mechanic	burglar	bungee jumper
Big Bad Wolf	disc jockey	lion tamer	sky diver
farmer	airline attendant	clown	secretary
disco dancer	opera singer	Princess Di	dentist
soldier	swimmer	acrobat	ice skater

What List

eating ice cream	typing	pulling a tooth
drowning in quicksand	playing football	sewing
skydiving	throwing snowballs	playing a drum
riding a camel	swallowing a sword	talking on the phone
ballet dancing	swallowing an oyster	painting your nails
being attacked by a shark	somersaulting	diving
roping a steer	handling a snake	walking a tightrope
changing a tire	making a movie	climbing a ladder
robbing a bank	riding an elephant	kayaking
cooking breakfast	snorkeling	driving a car
reading a scary book	eating a pickle	sneezing
swimming	climbing a mountain	boxing
running the 100 yard dash	frying chicken	roller blading
digging a grave	snowsledding	washing a car
washing your hair	bungee jumping	fishing
ice skating	giving a shot	yodeling
juggling	taking medicine	singing a song

Where List

in a cemetery	at a scary movie	in an elevator	in quicksand
in a hot air balloon	in prison	at a funny movie	in a race car
in the jungle	in an aerobics class	on a train	at the ballet
in a tunnel	at a rock concert	in a grocery store	in New York City
on a horse	in a submarine	at the beach	in the hospital
in an army tank	on top of Mt. Everest	on a raft	at a swimming pool
in the desert	at a tennis match	on the moon	in a baby buggy
in a shark's mouth	in a space shuttle	at a horse race	in a wheelchair
up a flagpole	on a subway	on an elephant	in the ocean
in the shower	at a flea market	at the zoo	on a surf board
in the army	in a cave	in a dense fog	in Hollywood
in Antarctica	on a trapeze	on a cliff edge	in the gym
on the ferris wheel	in a mine	at the North Pole	

Chapter 3

MOVEMENT

movement (müv ment) *n.* 1: a manner of moving 2: showing one's stuff 3: what Michael Jackson is full of 4: streamers and glittered canes 5: top hat and tails 6: energy 7: grace 8: fun.

Movement is to students what WD-40 is to gears. It takes the kinks out. Simply put, rhythm, dance, jumping, gliding, marching, and every other form of movement, is like a squirt of oil for a rusty Tin Man. It lubricates the joints, gets the blood flowing, providing oxygen and energy to the muscles, and lays the groundwork for a unique kind of creative expression.

Rhythm and movement are natural parts of life. Some people are more adept than others, but we are all born with the ability to sense rhythm and movement. We breathe. That is rhythmical. We walk, skip, skate, run, jump, and leap. That is movement. We add, subtract, multiply, and divide. That is patterning, which is basically rhythm. The human body is made for movement, its joints are in the right place. It is well balanced, and it can twirl and squat, soar and bend, stretch and recoil. It is the ultimate movement machine.

But wait, you say. If memory serves, the last time you went to a dance studio was when you were six. You also remember that the New York City Ballet never returned your calls. No matter. You certainly don't have to be Ginger Rogers or Fred Astaire to incorporate movement into your classroom. You're no Einstein, yet you teach math; you didn't win the Jonas Salk Award, yet you teach science, and you haven't climbed Mt. Everest, but you still teach geography. Get the picture?

So, put those tap shoes back in the closet and simply ask your students to walk. Have them walk normally, then with a limp, then like a bear, and then like a chicken. Now have them walk like a baby, an old man, backwards, with a skip, slowly, quickly, and blindfolded. You've brought movement into your classroom. Put on some music. Any kind. It doesn't matter. Now ask your students to move like clouds, raindrops, lightning, or wind. Have them spin their bodies like a hurricane. You've just incorporated movement into your science curriculum.

So buy yourself some scarves. Find some large pieces of flowing material. Collect some weird music. Push back the desks, and bring back your childhood.

Action Sentences

GRADE LEVEL: 3-6

MATERIALS: cassette player
appropriate upbeat music

AREA: open space

TIME NEEDED: 30 minutes

PURPOSE: To develop vocabulary, to practice action word usage, to express through creative movement, to strengthen teamwork skills, to generate an awareness of nuances in our language.

PROCEDURES:

1. Lead a discussion of the correct usage and importance of action words in our language.

2. Say a sentence such as, "I like to float like a cloud." Ask the class to name the action word in that sentence. Ask for volunteers to come to the front of the class and float like a cloud. Give other action words for volunteers to act out.

3. Ask students to find their own space in the room. Call out an action word and ask all the students to move as the word describes. Ask a student to use the word in a sentence. Repeat this activity several times until the children are clear about what kinds of movements are appropriate to the action words.

4. Divide the class into groups of three. Give each group a list of action words such as:

grow	fall	plop
spread	fly	blow
float	wobble	jab
twirl	leap	prance
scamper	settle	drop
bounce	explode	pause
glide	spin	shudder
bound	stretch	soar
collapse	drift	gallop
leap	drip	freeze
flick	slither	flutter
punch	kick	dive
press	fling	flip
sink	set	spring

5. Direct each group to select three action words, decide on what movement they will use for each action word, and make an *action sentence* by connecting three different movements together.

6. Each group will then have a chance to perform their action sentence for the rest of the class, who will try to guess what words are being used.

7. Put some upbeat music on, and let them begin.

ACADEMIC VARIATIONS:

Storytelling: Have the students make an action sentence move as the characters of a particular story would. For example, Goldilocks would *pounce* differently than Papa Bear, Mama Bear, or even Baby Bear.

Phonics—Blends: Call out a consonant blend. Students must think of an action word that begins with or contains that blend. For example, action words containing *st*: *stomp, stamp, sting, stick, stab.*

FLOURISHES:

For variety, use the tape you put together for the "Character Dancing" activity (pages 51-52). Have kids select one action word, for example, *plop*, and let them plop to the different musical moods.

Beat the Sticks

GRADE LEVEL: 5-6

MATERIALS: claves (rhythm sticks) or 12 inch wooden dowels

AREA: classroom

TIME NEEDED: 15 minutes

PURPOSE: To promote creative expression, to develop a steady beat, to reinforce listening skills, to acknowledge and experiment with patterns, to improve sequencing skills.

PROCEDURES:

1. Direct students to sit on the floor in a circle. Give each student two claves or two wooden dowels that have been cut into 12 inch lengths. Dowels of different diameters can be purchased very inexpensively at hardware stores or lumber yards. Dowels with one-half inch or one inch diameters are preferable, because they are easier to grip than those with smaller diameters.

2. To allow students time to warm up and get used to using the dowels, spend some time showing how the dowels should be held. For the right-handed person, the dowel in the left hand should be held lightly in the upturned palm of the hand. The dowel in the right hand should be held as though holding a normal stick. Left-handers will do the opposite. To strike, use the middle portion of the right dowel to strike the middle portion of the left dowel. This should be done without either dowel being gripped too firmly.

3. Once the correct grip has been established, give students a few moments to hit their sticks. This will alleviate some problems later on.

4. The teacher will begin making a steady beat with the dowels. Once that rhythm has been heard by the class, they will duplicate it. Do this call/response activity many times until students are responding together.

5. Now the teacher will play a pattern and call on students to answer it with either the same pattern or one of their own choosing.

6. Finally, students will, one at a time, begin playing their own patterns over and over until all of them are playing different beats at the same time. Then the first person will cease playing, as will each of the other students, one at a time, until the last person in the circle is the only one still playing.

7. To provide a sense of unity, and to ensure success, the teacher may want to give a four count between each student. This break gives the students a bit more preparation, and allows them to begin their own pattern at the proper time.

ACADEMIC VARIATION:

The skills of patience, timing, independence, cooperation, patterning, and so on can be integrated into all areas.

FLOURISHES:

Give students a piece of construction paper or tagboard. Ask them to use straight lines and make a *rhythm card* by drawing a beat on the paper. For example

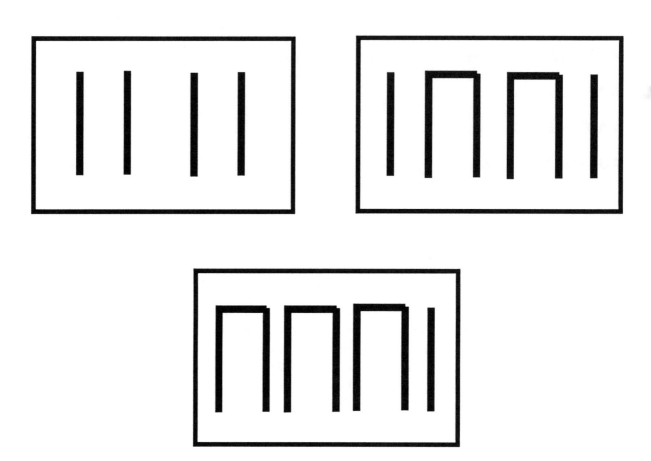

Sitting in a circle, students will hold up their rhythm cards, and have the other students make that pattern with their sticks. Another variation is to divide the students into two large groups who will sit on the floor facing each other. One group will line up several rhythm cards, so that only they can see them, and play them one at a time. Then the other group must echo what they have heard.

The Body Electric

GRADE LEVEL: 2-6

MATERIALS: cassette player
selection of upbeat music
tagboard pieces with different patterns and shapes drawn on them, such as:

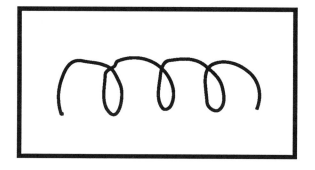

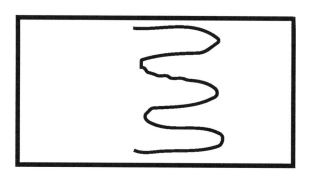

AREA: medium to large floor space preferred

TIME NEEDED: 10 minutes

PURPOSE: To enrich creative imagination, to use the human body to show energy and mood, to creatively express oneself through movement, to strengthen individual interpretation skills, to follow directions.

PROCEDURES:

1. Ask students to find their own space for this exercise. The teacher should be in a position to be seen by all of the students.

2. Begin playing music with a moderate, upbeat, or energetic sound.

3. Explain to the students that you are going to hold up cards that have designs and patterns on them. Ask the students to look at each design, and then move their bodies according to how the design or pattern makes them feel. Remind students that this is not a freeze exercise, but one requiring fluid movement. Stress that there is no right or wrong way to move, and that only individual interpretation matters.

ACADEMIC VARIATIONS:

Vowel Sounds: Write vowels on the cards and have the students move the way the vowel sound makes them feel. For example, short *a* might suggest little staccato movements, and long *o*, flowing movement.

Science: When studying sound or light waves, draw the pattern the wave would make. The students move their bodies following the wave pattern.

Weather: Draw or paste weather pictures on the cards. The students must then move as that weather pattern.

Math: Draw geometric shapes on the cards. Have the students move their body as that geometric shape or pattern.

FLOURISHES:

Give students scarves, and let them draw the different patterns and designs in the air. Better yet, let students, one at a time, come to a center space and draw something in the air with their scarves. The rest of the class must either try to reproduce the design with their own scarves, or draw the pattern on a piece of paper. The end product can be a great catalyst for a creative writing or abstract art activity.

Character Dancing

GRADE LEVEL: 4-6

MATERIALS: cassette player
cassette tapes with selections of different music genres (e.g., rock, classic, reggae, country, popular, gospel, rhythm and blues, opera, movie and TV themes, and scores)

AREA: large open space

TIME NEEDED: 10 minutes

PURPOSE: To reinforce characterization through body movement, to enhance listening skills, to develop an appreciation of different kinds of music, to promote individuality and self-concept, to motivate body awareness, to reinforce importance of personal space.

PROCEDURES:
1. Copy the following pages that contain lists of characters and objects needed for this activity. Cut those pages into strips and put the character and object names into a big hat or container.

2. Explain to the students that you are going to play different types of music—some fast, some slow, some with a heavy beat, some with a light beat—music that will produce different feelings when they hear it. Also explain that each student will pick a slip of paper that has the name of a person, animal, or object written on it.

3. When the music begins, the students must look at their character or object name, listen to the type of music that is being played, and dance or move the way that particular character or object would. For example, how would Tarzan move to a country music beat?

4. When the music changes, the students should pick another character name out of the hat and dance or move as that character would. Continue picking new names as long as the music changes. Each music selection shouldn't last more than 10-12 seconds.

5. It is important for the teacher to model this activity before the class begins.

ACADEMIC VARIATIONS:

Social Studies: Give groups of children an era in history to research. Part of the research should include the music, culture, and etiquette of that period. The characters and objects on the slips should reflect the culture of the different time periods researched. Students can dance or move to the music the way someone from that time period would.

Alphabet Review: Students must think of and dance or move to things that begin alphabetically (e.g., *a*nt, *b*utterfly, *c*lam, *d*inosaur, and so on).

Science: Have students pick a geographic area of the world (for example, Antarctica). Have them dance or move the way creatures or objects (such as iceberg, penguins, crevasse) from that area would move.

Environmental Education: While studying a unit on pollution, for example, have students become inanimate objects that pollute (garbage, old tires, aluminum cans). Have them show, through movement, how those particular things devastate the environment if they are not cleaned up. For example, one "tire" can roll and rest on the floor. Another and another and yet another tire will "roll" to the spot and pile on top of each other.

FLOURISHES:

Science/Health: When teaching the circulatory system, let each student select a character (e.g., old woman, teenager, football player, baby, or corpse). Play the kinds of music mentioned above and ask the students to stay in character and dance or move accordingly. Then have students take their pulse. Make a graph of the ages of the characters as they relate to the heartbeats. Discuss how age relates to energy, why pulse rates are different in people whose ages and occupations are different, and what consequences, if any, a fast or slow heartbeat has on certain individuals.

Character and
Object List

teenager	stapler	beach ball	skier
chicken	spoiled brat	rainbow	book
Cowardly Lion	Pacific Ocean	newborn baby	ice skater
former President Bush	Shirley Temple	Christmas tree	typewriter
John Wayne	scissors	watermelon	Joe Montana
jeep	shadow	Charlie Chaplin	Snoopy
rope	Batman	aspirin tablet	human heart
lobster	king	swing	grandfather clock
your mother	matador	hand puppet	lightning
Popeye	Rapunzel	pregnant woman	Superman
whirling dervish	monkey	puff fish	Father Time
jack-in-the-box	camel	mouse	Agent 007
E.T.	Tarzan	ghost	minister
robot	corpse	kangaroo	nurse
pencil sharpener	spy	dog dish	snake
Big Bird	sea captain	raindrop	lamp
Michael Jordan	tidal wave	Little Mermaid	stop sign
Red Riding Hood	volcano	copy machine	bell
whale	sun	munchkin	aspen tree
acrobat	moon	Cinderella	Alka-Seltzer
Golden Gate Bridge	clown	Ben Franklin	kite
TV set	Ringo Starr	Robin Hood	rock
diamond ring	computer	North Wind	electric eel
deck of cards	pencil	mad dog	hat
Superman	fish	quicksand	computer
old person	violin	Hercules	drag racer
Queen of England	eraser	fountain pen	golf ball
Marilyn Monroe	sea otter	kiwi fruit	snowflake
eagle	super glue	fork	Frankenstein
rock 'n' roller	rock climber	Madonna	earthquake
tornado	puppy	Dracula	King Arthur
bubble	flower	Dumbo	Snow White
octopus	elephant	sneakers	shark
your father	clam	marbles	sponge
tennis racket	rocking chair	Saturn	willow tree
porpoise	troll	crayon	rabbit
vampire	submarine	iceberg	tap dancer
pogo stick	alligator	Mary Poppins	

Dance Maps

GRADE LEVEL: 3-6

MATERIALS: construction paper
   markers or crayons

AREA: open floor space

TIME NEEDED: 45 minutes

PURPOSE: To read maps and create original map legends, to develop creative expression through movement, to practice problem solving, to demonstrate following directions, to enhance cooperative learning, to build self-esteem.

PROCEDURES:

1. In the room in which you will be doing this activity, place cards on the walls to designate North, South, East, and West.

2. Divide students into groups of three, four, or five, and give each group a piece of construction paper, and a marker or crayon.

3. Using their knowledge of maps, legends, and symbols, students will create a dance map making original symbols for different ways of moving around the room. The object of this activity is for the students to decide on a starting and ending point in the room, and navigate with different movement steps between those two points. A dance map might look like this:

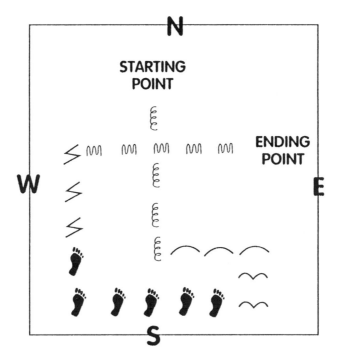

The legend and symbols would look like this:

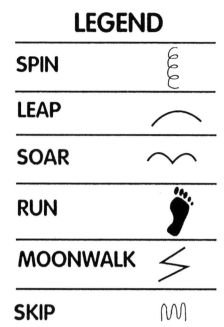

LEGEND

SPIN	
LEAP	
SOAR	
RUN	
MOONWALK	
SKIP	

4. Upon completion of their dance maps, students will move as the map tells them to. In reading the above map, for example, the students will:

   a. Begin at the starting point.
   b. Spin south four steps or beats.
   c. Leap east three steps or beats.
   d. Soar south two steps or beats.
   e. Run west five steps or beats.
   f. Moonwalk north three steps or beats.
   g. Skip east five steps or beats.

5. When all groups have followed their maps, let them exchange maps and follow each other's maps. This time, add music to spice up the presentations.

ACADEMIC VARIATIONS:

Science: In studying the digestive or circulatory systems, have students create dance maps to show how blood travels through the body, or where a piece of pizza goes when it is eaten.

Social Studies: As a culmination to a unit on the Westward Movement, students may create a dance map that shows the different hardships encountered by the pioneers. Events such as starvation, raids, floods, diseases, cold weather, could be described through movement.

Reading/Creative Writing: Select a favorite children's story. Students will develop a dance map that retells the story through action. Be sure to stress beginning, middle, and end of the story in the dance map.

FLOURISHES:

Go out to the playground. Divide the students into groups, give each group an object (e.g., ruler, pencil, small ball, box of paper clips, or comb), and ask the groups to hide their objects, being careful not to let the members of the other groups see where the objects are hidden. Now ask the groups to make a dance map that will lead others to the *hidden treasure.* Remind students that since this activity is done outdoors, the dance map can have more symbols, longer steps, and can be made a bit more complicated.

Give your own students a chance to follow the maps, then invite another class to try to find one of the hidden objects.

Have a picnic on the playground and make a map that shows where you have hidden a treat for the class.

Flashlight Dance

GRADE LEVEL: 1-5

MATERIALS: 1 flashlight per child
colored cellophane paper attached to the end of each flashlight

AREA: large open space such as gym, cafeteria, activity room, or classroom with desks pushed back

TIME NEEDED: 15 minutes

PURPOSE: To review vocabulary words, spelling words, letters of the alphabet, geometric shapes; to discover creative expression through movement.

PROCEDURES:

1. Find a room that can be darkened.

2. Give each child a flashlight which has colored cellophane attached to the end. Colored cellophane rolls can be found at art supply stores, office supply stores, and some arts and crafts stores. Plastic wrap also comes in colors, and can be found at your neighborhood grocery store.

3. Turn off lights, turn on flashlights, and direct students to:

   a. Trace the shape of letters of the alphabet on the floor, the ceiling, each other's backs, in the air, or wherever else they want.
   b. Form a circle and use their flashlights to make geometric shapes, such as circles, squares, rectangles, triangles, and ovals in the air, on the ceiling, on the wall, or on a body part.
   c. Listen to spelling or vocabulary words and write the words in cursive.
   d. Observe something on another person like clothing or jewelry, and spell out that object.

ACADEMIC VARIATIONS:

Storytelling: To enhance the telling of a story, use flashlights to produce different moods. Flashlights also work well to set the mood for holiday stories, especially ones pertaining to Halloween.

Science: In studying constellations, assign each student a section of the night sky. By pricking pin holes in dark construction paper put over the flashlight, students will be able to create their particular constellation, and beam it on the ceiling of a dark room. The class can guess which constellation it is, and where it goes in relation to the other constellations.

FLOURISHES:

Have students stand in a circle with their colored flashlights. Play some Pointer Sisters or Aretha Franklin, and allow students to do improvisational movement in a follow-the-leader format, with the teacher leading. Continue in a circle or allow line dancing. Either way, the kids love this one. Now break students into groups and give them time to choreograph their own routines using flashlights. Five or six minutes is enough time for preparation. Give them a scarf as a prop for the other hand, and see what happens!

Hand Dancing

GRADE LEVEL: 3-6

MATERIALS: dark sheet or cloth
white gloves
heavy-duty yarn or twine
clothespins
cassette player
appropriate music

AREA: corner of classroom

TIME NEEDED: 15 minutes

PURPOSE: To promote creative expression, to enhance communication skills, to promote cooperative learning.

PROCEDURES:

1. Take an old sheet and dye it black, or buy black remnants from a fabric store and sew them together. Stretch yarn or twine across the corner of your classroom. Pin the black cloth to the yarn with clothespins, or fold the top of the sheet over the yarn and staple it all the way across. Now cut two vertical slits in the cloth about waist high on your students and 10 inches apart. Cut as many of these double slits as your width of sheet will allow.

2. Give students two white gloves each. Ask a few of them to stand behind the black cloth and gently stick a gloved hand through each slit. Some students may opt to sit on stools or in chairs rather than stand.

3. Put some upbeat music on, and let the students do their own improvisational hand dance. The only things that show are the white hands, and in a dark room, with a spotlight of some sort, this activity is exciting to participate in, and to watch. (The spotlight can be a filmstrip projector light, a heavy-duty flashlight, or an automotive light.)

ACADEMIC VARIATIONS:

Oral Reading: When reading a story, assign different characters to the students. The student's hand(s) will become the character and will act out the part similar to a puppet.

Language Arts: Use the black cloth as a puppet theater. Allow the students to make finger puppets and act out original stories or poems.

Role-playing: With discipline situations, playground rule infractions, or classroom management problems, allow the students to use this as an arena to dialogue and solve those problems in a nonthreatening way.

Social Studies: Let the kids make up their own white glove or puppet scenarios that coincide with what they are studying (e.g., community helpers, pioneers, pilgrims, transportation, natural resources).

FLOURISHES:

Divide your students into groups of four or five, depending on how many want to work together. Give them a day or so to choose the song they'll lip-sync. Show the kids how to make a fist face. (Make a fist and use markers to paint lips around the perimeter of your thumb and index finger, add eyes, a nose, and, Voila! a face with no teeth.)

Explain that their fist faces are going to be the performers who will be lip-syncing the song. Remind them that each group member should play a part. Allow rehearsal time. (Kids can bring their own cassette players for this activity.)

Invite another class to watch. Don't forget to plug in the video camera.

Paper Plate Dancing

GRADE LEVEL: K-6

MATERIALS: paper plates
upbeat music

AREA: open space with smooth floor or indoor/outdoor carpet

TIME NEEDED: 5 minutes

PURPOSE: To express creative body movement, to develop awareness of personal space.

PROCEDURES:

1. Take the class to an area that has a smooth floor. Give the students two paper plates. Direct them to put a foot on each plate.

2. Turn up some fun dance music and let the kids go in their own improvisational dances. Remind students that sliding and running into others is inappropriate behavior.

3. When the dance is over, spend some time on questions like, "What felt good about doing that?" or "Which movement was the most fun?" or "In what other ways could we use the plates to express ourselves?"

4. The last statement could be an introduction to using the plates as hand props for another dance. Let the kids experiment.

FLOURISHES:

The *Bele Kawe* is an African dance that can be done with paper plate masks. The dance steps can be found in Phyllis S. Weikart's *Teaching Movement and Dance* (High/Scope Press, 1982), and the music can be found in the *Rhythmically Moving* (High Scope Educational Research, 1983) tapes that go along with her dances. If you have access to the dance steps but not the music, try to locate music that has an African beat, and allow the students to make up their own dance using handmade paper plate masks in the dance.

If you are in the middle of an environmental unit, find some music suggestive of animals, and let kids make animal masks to use with an original dance. This idea has many possibilities and you'll be surprised at how focused children can be with this type of activity.

Chapter 4

PANTOMIME

pantomime (pan to mīm) *n.* 1: a performance presented through bodily or facial movements 2: how Marcel Marceau takes care of his mortgage payments 3: a teaching tool that succeeds with almost all of your students 4: a solution to your Open House dilemma 5: energy 6: fun.

Pantomime is a dramatic art form that almost everybody can do. You don't have to be Marcel Marceau or Robert Shields to pretend to be doing something well enough that other people can guess what it is. Some students find it less intimidating to explain their ideas non-verbally at first. This is one reason why the inclusion of pantomime into your daily curriculum is so valuable. It gives those students a chance to be "heard."

Pantomime fits into the elementary school curriculum at every level. Ask your first graders to pantomime different animals in different habitats, and let your third graders pantomime emotions. Have your fifth graders pantomime things indigenous to certain parts of the United States. Let your sixth graders pantomime the water cycle. The ideas are endless, and the result is usually success.

Pantomime can be done improvisationally, that is, quickly and without much practice. Or you can ask students to prepare more by thinking of a pantomime scenario in which the entire piece has a beginning, middle, and end. Personally, we think it works best when there is not much forethought. Just present the problem, and let the students take it from there.

In many of the pantomime exercises in this book, we suggest having the students use pantomime first, then having them use the same actions with words. Stretching pantomime situations into verbal scenes works especially well for developing listening and communication skills.

Although makeup is not necessary when doing pantomime, allowing the kids to dabble with clown white, cold cream, baby powder, cotton balls, and black eyeliner can often be an added stimulus. It's a good way to introduce the concept of masks, and when and why we wear them.

During a pantomime program, have the performers put on their mime masks in front of the children explaining, as they go, what they are doing and why. This can lead to a wonderful discussion regarding communication, freedom of expression, and what it takes to become someone or something else.

After all, we all need a little clown white in our lives once in a while.

Big and Little

GRADE LEVEL: K-6

MATERIALS: none

AREA: classroom

TIME NEEDED: 10 minutes

PURPOSE: To review opposites in a visual way, to demonstrate definitions through body movement, to reinforce nonverbal communication, to develop self-esteem.

PROCEDURES:

1. On individual index cards, make a list of words or paste pictures of objects such as:

   rock
   animal
   water
   building
   furniture
   food
   tree
   musical instrument
   transportation

2. Ask students to pair up. Have one partner demonstrate *big* and one *small* versions of the words on the cards. Hold up a card and allow students to act out the word at the size they've been assigned. For example, if the word is *rock*, one student could demonstrate big by climbing a huge mountain. Another student might demonstrate small by playing on the beach building a sand castle.

3. A class discussion should follow each presentation, focusing on the differences between the two descriptions. Students may want to describe or name other objects in between a grain of sand and a mountain in size. One such object could be a boulder.

4. It is important to emphasize that the pantomime should make sense, be as complete as possible, and focus on the particular size being described.

ACADEMIC VARIATIONS:

Visual Arts: Give students a piece of construction paper on which is written a word. Students must then draw a picture incorporating big and little buildings in one scene that makes sense.

Social Studies: Give students opposite words like *big/little, fast/slow, easy/hard,* and *long/short.* They must use these words to compare aspects of a subject. For example, when studying transportation, students can discuss the differences in the modes of transportation that were deemed fast (e.g., railroads, airplanes, automobiles, and chariots) and those that were thought of as slower (e.g., wagons, horses, steamboats, and rafts).

FLOURISHES:

    Give students art paper with two similar figures on it, one large and one small. Have students draw a picture using these figures as beginning points. Example:

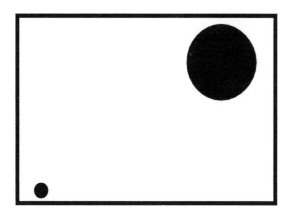

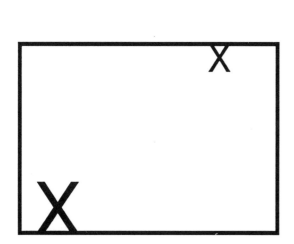

    Emphasize that they are to keep in mind the large and small in their pictures. Now pass the completed pictures around, and let other students add an original story.

Connection

GRADE LEVEL: 3-6

MATERIALS: none

AREA: classroom

TIME NEEDED: 25 minutes

PURPOSE: To develop cooperative learning skills, to practice sequencing, to communicate verbally and nonverbally, to draw conclusions, to think logically using higher order thinking, to speak spontaneously.

PROCEDURES:

1. Divide the class into groups of five or more students. Have the groups select leaders. The leaders decide on a theme for the group to act out, but do not tell the group members what the theme is.

2. A leader from one group goes to the front of the class and begins to act out one thing that would relate to the chosen theme.

3. The rest of the group, one at a time, joins the leader by doing something that relates to what the leader is doing. For example, if the leader is pretending to fish, the second child might bait a hook, the third child might try to start a boat motor, the fourth child might try to get the fish off the hook, and the fifth child might become the fish that is being caught.

4. A suggestion is for a group to do the exercise nonverbally first, then act out the same scene with dialogue.

5. End the exercise with all the students connecting in some way to a large theme such as a circus. Students will enter the area one at a time, and pantomime something that can be seen or done at a circus. A discussion on the importance of communication should follow this activity.

6. Some suggested scenarios are:

sunbathing	surgery	grocery store
building a house	bowling	golfing
playing tennis	cooking dinner	horse racing
preparing for a vacation	playing baseball	going to the library
watching a movie	doctor's office	picnic

ACADEMIC VARIATIONS:

Social Studies: Act out scenes that have occurred in history or in current events. For example, a pioneer family moving west, or archaeologists at a dig.

Math Word Problems: Each group decides on a story problem to act out. Group members discuss who does what and in what order. After presenting the nonverbal action story problem, the rest of the class must guess the math problem and come up with the solution.

Science: When studying the systems of the body, have each group member act out the functions of that particular system. For example, if pantomiming the digestive system, the first person might bite into an imaginary hamburger, chew, and swallow; the second person would squeeze his hands together to show throat function; the third person jiggle like a stomach squashing food around, and so on.

Desk Pantomimes

GRADE LEVEL: K-6

MATERIALS: none

AREA: school desk or table

TIME NEEDED: 5 minutes

PURPOSE: To promote creative expression, to follow directions, to describe details nonverbally.

PROCEDURES:

1. Ask the students to sit comfortably at their desks and use all parts of their bodies as they pretend to:

type on a computer	look at self in a mirror
sew on a button	listen to crickets
toss paper in the trash	relax on a boat
dream	blow a bubble
saw a log	eat a popsicle
think	go to sleep and snore
watch a fly buzz around head	ride a bicycle
look through binoculars	make a snowball
fly a paper airplane	rock a baby

2. For variety, you may want to ask the students to do the activity nonverbally at first, then verbally, to emphasize the importance of different methods of communication.

3. Allow time for individual students to think up more desk pantomimes they may want to share with the rest of the class.

ACADEMIC VARIATIONS:

This activity is a good warm-up to any pantomime activity you are planning on doing in science, social studies, language arts, or other subjects. It focuses students at the beginning of the school day, and it works well as a wrap-up at the end of the day.

FLOURISHES:

Since the kids are at their desks anyway, ask them to make it a prop in their pantomime. For example, it could be a cave for a sleeping bear, a cockpit for a pilot, or a race car for an Indy 500 driver. A desk makes a great donkey for pantomiming the Aesop Fable, "The Miller, His Son, and His Donkey."

Exaggeration

GRADE LEVEL: 2-6

MATERIALS: none

AREA: classroom

TIME NEEDED: 15 minutes

PURPOSE: To promote creative expression, to practice nonverbal communication, to understand and demonstrate the concept of small and large, to demonstrate progression.

PROCEDURES:

1. Lead the class in a discussion of the definition of the word *exaggerate*. A student may want to look it up in the dictionary and read the definition aloud. Ask several volunteers to come to the front of the class and exaggerate laughing, crying, shaking, blowing a bubble, and carrying a book.

2. Now ask all of the students to exaggerate the same thing together.

3. Divide students into groups of five or six. The first student begins by pantomiming an action or an object. The next person in the group will exaggerate that action or object and make it bigger. The next person in the group will continue to exaggerate even more, until the last student in the group is exaggerating to such a degree that it may take all of the members of the group to help with the action or object. An example might be someone tying shoelaces normally. The next student must lift the shoelaces with two hands. The next student may have to struggle to lift the shoelaces then toss them over a shoulder because they are so big and heavy. The next student may have to get a forklift to lift the shoelaces to be able to tie them, and so on.

4. Here are some suggested actions or objects that might be exaggerated:

   piece of string
   putting on a pair of gloves
   petting the dog
   seed growing
   worm
   drinking a glass of water
   mowing the lawn
   bouncing a ball
   erasing on a piece of paper
   frying an egg

ACADEMIC VARIATIONS:

Reading: Have students sit in a circle on the floor. One student begins telling a story, original or not. Going around the room, each student will exaggerate and embellish the story as it is being told. The point here is not so much continuity, but the ability to broaden the story to wide proportions.

Creative Writing: For the older students, give them two objects that are similar, but vary in size. For example, *pebble/mountain, piece of hair/cable that holds the Golden Gate Bridge together, weed/tree, pond/ocean, small toy truck/monster truck.* Have them write a story that revolves around how the first of the two objects become the second object.

FLOURISHES:

Four students line up in front of the class. They are not allowed to discuss strategy or maneuvers with each other. The teacher will call out a word. For example, if the word is *clock*, one student begins doing something having to do with a tiny timepiece, like listening to a wristwatch to see if it is still working and making appropriate comments. The next student picks up a bedside clock and rewinds it while commenting appropriately. The third student goes up to a grandfather clock and makes the pendulum swing commenting on the action, and the last student stands in front of Big Ben, in London, and comments on time.

Human Alphabet

GRADE LEVEL: K-6

MATERIALS: none

AREA: open floor space

TIME NEEDED: 20 minutes

PURPOSE: To review letters of the alphabet in a creative way, to practice spelling words, to visualize prefixes and suffixes, to work cooperatively.

PROCEDURES:

1. Allow students to find a space in an open area, and explain that they will be using their bodies to make different words and letters of the alphabet. Explain also that they are free to do this activity standing, lying down, or sitting on the floor.

2. The following letters or words can be formed thus:

individually	E, F, I, J, K, L, P, R, S, T, V, X, Z
with partners	A, B, C, D, E, G, H, M, N, O, Q, U, W
groups of three	IT, UP, SAP, SIT, NO, TOY, GOT, SAY
groups of four	SAIL, WET, ROT, PAT, PIT, LET
groups of five	GONE, LOT, MAN, RAW, MEAN, BARK
groups of six	WHAT, OCEAN, BUS, POTATO, FLOOD

3. When the students have practiced forming letters and words using groups of five or six students, let them think of their own word and shape it. Other groups must try to spell the newly formed words.

ACADEMIC VARIATIONS:

Phonics: Use human alphabets to review prefixes, suffixes, dropping the silent *e*, digraphs, changing *y* to *i* and adding *es*, and so on.

Spelling: This is an active way of reviewing spelling words and vocabulary words.

Math Problems: Students use their bodies to answer math problems given by the teacher. This activity can also be used to create math equations, or to demonstrate carrying, borrowing, and place value, among other things.

FLOURISHES:

When studying measurements, take the kids outside on the playground, and let all but one or two students make a single giant letter of the alphabet. The two not participating in the letter measure the height of that letter in inches, feet, yards, and miles.

Musical Sticks

GRADE LEVEL: K-6

MATERIALS: cassette player
selection of lively music
tagboard pieces or large posterboard sheets with different stick figure shapes drawn
on them such as:

AREA: medium to large floor space

TIME NEEDED: 10 minutes

PURPOSE: To reinforce following directions, to express creativity through movement, to show how different body postures can indicate different moods, to enhance observation skills.

PROCEDURES:

1. Ask the students to find an appropriate place in the room that will become their own space for this activity. You should stand where the entire class can see you.

2. Begin playing music with a lively beat.

3. Explain to students that you are going to hold up cards that have funny stick figure drawings on them. Their job is to try to imitate the figures on the cards. Remind students that if the stick figures have an arm or leg sticking up, students should note which arm or leg is being held up. (Some students mirror what they see.)

4. Give students an opportunity to hold up the cards.

ACADEMIC VARIATIONS:

Phonics: Use cards with blends, digraphs, and initial consonants on them. Students make their bodies in the shape of an object that uses those letters. For example, if the blend is *pl*, students can pantomime a plate, pliers, or planet.

Emotions: With stick figure emotional faces, students must shape an emotional body to go with the expressions. For example, a sad face and a droopy body.

FLOURISHES:

Give students each a piece of white sketch paper. Let them draw their own musical stick figures, reminding them to shape their stick body as creatively as possible, making sure a live body can imitate it. Then let them take turns holding up their cards for the rest of the class to try to imitate. Don't forget the music. It's what sets the mood.

Narrative Pantomime

GRADE LEVEL: 1-6

MATERIALS: cassette player
slow instrumental music
white gloves
selection of children's books

AREA: floor space

TIME NEEDED: 20 minutes

PURPOSE: To describe characters through hand movements, to show creative expression, to retell a story, to distinguish differences in character traits, to focus on different body parts.

PROCEDURES:

1. Give students a pair of white gloves each, and have them sit on the floor facing you.

2. Explain that you are going to ask them to show you different things by pantomiming with just their hands. If you ask them to pantomime *snowball*, students pretend to pack a snowball with their hands and hold it up for you to see.

3. Here are some suggested warm-ups for pantomiming with hands:

strong hands	a dog burying a bone
weak hands	someone begging for food
small hands	hands on a hot day
large hands	hands on a cold day
scared hands	happy hands
a snake climbing a tree	someone holding a flower
a bear after hibernation	someone putting a flower in a vase
a caterpillar on a leaf	your father's hands
a butterfly	your mother's hands
a witch's hands	your hands
a spider weaving his web	

4. Play slow instrumental music to enhance the mood of the class and to lessen noise level. The music helps the students concentrate.

5. Find a children's story or fable with two characters. Have students pantomime a character with each hand. Read the story aloud as students act out the characters' parts with their hands. A good two-character story may be:

The Snake and the Ant

by Martha Brady

(Adapted from *The Mouse and the Flea*, an Alaskan folktale.)

Deep in the forest where many things go unnoticed, there lived a snake and an ant. The snake lived in a long, long tunnel deep in the ground and never came up out of the tunnel unless he was sure there was nobody around.

His only friend, the ant, lived underneath a piece of curled bark on the side of an old oak tree and spent most of his day running up and down the bark looking for things to carry and move.

Now, these two were very good friends and spent quite a bit of time together. Sometimes Mr. Ant would hop down into Mr. Snake's tunnel and sit on Mr. Snake's back and scratch it when Mr. Snake's scales got a bit itchy. Other times, Mr. Ant would make sure the coast was clear and ask Mr. Snake to come out of the tunnel so that Mr. Ant could sunbathe on Mr. Snake's back. Now this was true friendship.

Often if Mr. Ant needed to go across the forest to visit relatives or go to the store, Mr. Snake would wiggle out of his tunnel and slither up the tree where Mr. Ant would then jump on Mr. Snake's head and off they would go. Sometimes Mr. Snake would make a path in the soft dirt with his body so that Mr. Ant would have a newly built road to travel when carrying especially heavy objects to his home. Many times, Mr. Ant would find bits of food from the forest floor and would push and roll them down into Mr. Snake's tunnel. Mr. Snake stayed well fed because of this kind act. This was indeed a glorious friendship.

The two spent quite a bit of time together and this sometimes caused Mr. Ant and Mr. Snake to get mad and lose their tempers. When this happened, the two friends would often do unkind things to each other. One day when Mr. Snake didn't want to come out of his hole to take Mr. Ant across the forest to a friend's house, Mr. Ant called all of his relatives to come push hundreds of small stones, twigs, and grains of sand into Mr. Snake's tunnel. Mr. Snake had to work for a long time to clear his path to the top of the hole. Another time when Mr. Ant was working hard to carry small pieces of leaves to his home, Mr. Snake stretched across Mr. Ant's path and made him detour completely around his body. This took a long time and Mr. Ant was very tired when he finally arrived home.

As the weeks went by, the unkind acts between the two creatures continued. After each instance, Mr. Ant and Mr. Snake would apologize for their misbehavior and return to being good friends. However, in short time, they would get into another argument and once again think of ways to trick each other. Soon the other insects and animals stayed as far away from the two as possible, vowing to have nothing more to do with them.

One morning as Mr. Ant slowly dragged a piece of brightly colored string to his home, Mr. Wren, looking for just the right material to complete his nest, saw the string, swooped down, picked up the string with Mr. Ant clinging onto it, and flew toward the very top of the tree which contained his nest. As the bird soared upward, a strong gust of wind blew the string out of his mouth and the string, helped along by the wind, floated lazily along until it fell gently down into a forest pond.

Mr. Ant, realizing that he was in imminent danger because he could not swim, clung onto the piece of string for dear life, yelling at the top of his little lungs. Fish swam by and laughed, but did nothing to help Mr. Ant because they thought it was yet another trick by Mr. Snake. Mr. Frog, who was sitting on a lily pad in the pond, didn't even raise his eyebrows when he heard Mr. Ant hollering for help. Mr. Ant continued to yell, but no one paid any attention.

Soon the string became so soaked with water that it slowly began to sink, leaving Mr. Ant flailing his legs desperately with nothing to grab onto to save him. Believing all was lost, Mr. Ant thought about his friend Mr. Snake and all of the bad things the two had done to each other over the years. "Oh, if only I had one more chance, I would never ever do anything bad to my friend again. I would think of ways to be kind and helpful, not mean and spiteful. I would be the best friend a snake could have," sputtered the ant as he slipped under the water.

Suddenly, Mr. Ant found himself lying on something very firm and that something was pushing him up out of the water. Up, up, up to fresh air and sky and breeze.

Gasping, Mr. Ant looked around and saw, to his amazement, that he was lying on the back of Mr. Snake who was stretched out on top of the bobbing water. "How did you ever find me? How did you know I was here?" asked Mr. Ant.

"Well," said Mr. Snake, "I saw that old wren flying off with that piece of string and I knew how you loved leaves and twigs and string for yourself, so when I saw the wind take that string away, I just figured you were probably holding onto it real tight. And, because you are my friend, well, here I am."

As the two made their way toward the bank of the pond, Mr. Ant said, "You know, Mr. Snake, I've been thinking."

"Me too," responded Mr. Snake.

And the two friends looked at each other, smiled, and continued their journey toward home.

ACADEMIC VARIATIONS:

Health: Pair students up. Ask them to give an oral report on some aspect of health (e.g., smoking, drugs, or good nutrition). One person gives the report, the other acts it out through hand pantomime.

Science or Social Studies: Divide students into groups of four or five. Give each group a topic to discuss. As a group, students act out their discussion with their hands.

FLOURISHES:

Have students select their favorite children's book, nursery rhyme, or fairy tale. Have them tell the story nonverbally, using their hands. The other students must guess which story they are telling.

Paintbrush Spelling

GRADE LEVEL: K-6

MATERIALS: none

AREA: classroom

TIME NEEDED: 5 minutes

PURPOSE: To review shapes of letters, to practice spelling words.

PROCEDURES:

1. Direct students to find a space in the room.

2. Direct students to dip their brushes into their buckets and paint a word in large bold strokes, in the air, using an imaginary paint bucket and paintbrush. For example, *LOVE*.

3. When the students have finished painting each letter with their brushes, allow them to pantomime by:

   hanging on the *L;*
   stepping through the *O;*
   sticking their heads through the *V;*
   sitting on the middle part of the *E.*

ACADEMIC VARIATIONS:

This basic form of pantomime can also be used in reviewing spelling words, vocabulary words, the use of blends, digraphs, parts of speech, or in the writing of numbers or math problems.

FLOURISHES:

Take your kindergartners or first graders outside and give them real paintbrushes, some real finger or watercolor paints, and let them draw huge letters of the alphabet that can be made into faces (see page 77).

Once they have done that, why not let them tell the short life story of each face they have made.

ALPHABET FACES

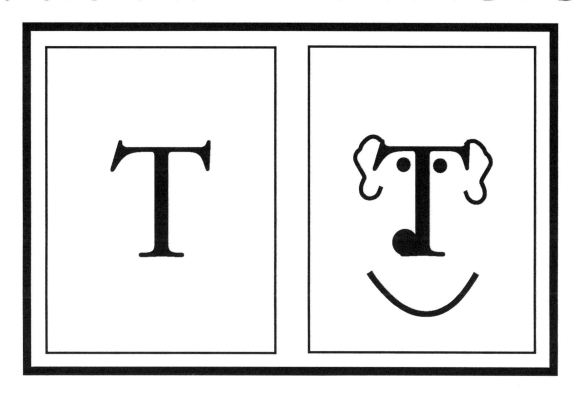

Pantomime Skits

GRADE LEVEL: 3-6

MATERIALS: clown white makeup
moderately upbeat music
white gloves (optional)
black turtleneck (optional)

AREA: classroom, gym

TIME NEEDED: 45 minutes

PURPOSE: To communicate using nonverbal skills, to strengthen teamwork, to develop creative expression, to enhance self-esteem.

PROCEDURES:

The following are self-contained pantomime skits, that require students to stay in character throughout the exercise. These are just suggestions of how each skit can be pantomimed. Remember that your students' original ideas can be much better.

The Butterflies

Four students. One person holds a pretend bag. Three students, one at a time, reach into the bag, retrieve a butterfly, and let it land on parts of their bodies. The three students let the butterflies loose, watching as they fly off into the distance. Butterflies are made by forming thumb and index finger into a circle, and fluttering the three remaining fingers by twisting the wrist rapidly.

Shoe Salesperson

Three students. One person is the shoe salesperson who is busy straightening up a pretend box of shoes. The first customer enters and asks for shoes. The shoe salesperson looks at the customer's foot and shows with her hands the size he needs. He nods. She puts the shoes on his feet. He pays and walks out normally. The second customer walks in haughtily. She asks for a pair of shoes. The salesperson looks at the foot and with her hands shows that she needs a really large size. She shakes her head and shows a small size. The salesperson shows a larger size. The customer shakes her head. This continues, and the customer steadfastly refuses to take anything but a teeny-tiny shoe size. The salesperson agrees, reluctantly, and puts shoes on the customer's feet with great difficulty. She pays and walks out, taking small painful steps.

The Rock

Four students. Three students, pretending to be big and strong, try to lift a heavy, imaginary rock to no avail. Each struggles, gets red in the face, and tries several times but cannot budge the rock. The fourth student, who pretends to be small and weak, sees the rock, picks it up with no effort, and walks off.

The Pickle

One student. The student goes to a pretend refrigerator, looks in, finds and takes out a pickle jar, unscrews the jar, takes out a large pickle, bites into it, makes a horrendous face, slams the pickle jar down on the cabinet, and walks off.

The Boat

Three students. One at a time the students climb into a small boat. They begin to paddle smoothly. Suddenly, one student notices a leak in the bottom of the boat. All begin to paddle furiously. They notice that more water is coming up through the leak. They throw the oars away, grab buckets, and begin to bail the water out. This does not work, either, so all three hold their noses, wave goodbye to the audience, and slowly lean back and down into the boat.

The Museum

Six students. Four students space themselves side by side and freeze their bodies into pieces of sculpture. One student enters with a museum catalog in hand. The student looks at the sculptures one at a time. As the student moves from one sculpture to another, the pieces of sculptures follow that student with their eyes. Once the visitor leaves, the four sculptures dance and move around crazily, without making any noise. Another museum visitor enters with a catalog. At the instant the second viewer comes into view, the sculptures freeze into their original stances.

Here are titles of other short pantomime skits. Let kids use their imagination and create their own skits to these titles or other titles.

The Rope	The Balloons
The Seeds	The Drip
The Glass Wall	The Window
The Table	The Ice Cream Store
The Gossiper	The Piano Player
The Bus	The Bowling Alley
The Robots	

FLOURISHES:

If your class is studying careers and community, have kids pick a community helper, such as a fireman, do a pantomime skit that puts the fireman in a typical situation. Have students pantomime several activities a fireman performs (e.g., climbing a ladder, holding a hose, and riding in back of the truck), mixing in one unusual activity for a fireman (e.g., operating on a patient). See if the rest of the class can pick out the activity that doesn't fit.

RhymeAct

GRADE LEVEL: 4-6

MATERIALS: none

AREA: classroom

TIME NEEDED: 15 minutes

PURPOSE: To develop rhyming skills, to review word definitions, to pantomime word meanings.

PROCEDURES:
1. Ask four students at a time to stand in front of the class.

2. The teacher will whisper the same word into the ear of each student.

3. At a signal, each student must act out a word that rhymes with the word whispered by the teacher. For example, if the word is *dead*, students may want to act out *bed, read, fed,* or *led*. Students must act out their rhyming words one at a time. No two students can act out the same word. If two students think of the same word, the second person to act it out must change words.

4. The rest of the class must guess what the rhyming words are. A student who successfully guesses the word, gets to replace the student whose word was guessed, and the teacher whispers another word.

    Some suggested words include:

feel	lake	lip
cat	keep	sky
wave	kite	blue
Ted	cake	run
rot	glow	

ACADEMIC VARIATIONS:

Synonyms or Vocabulary Definitions: The teacher gives a definition. The students must act out the word that goes with that definition. If the definition applies to several words or synonyms, the students must show the nuances needed to make their particular word different from the other synonyms. If the definition is "to look quickly," student choices might be *glance, peek,* or *glimpse*. When acting out those words, the students should do so in a way to differentiate between words.

Science, Social Studies, or Geography Vocabulary Review: The students draw cards with scientific, social studies, or geographic terms on them related to the topic being studied. Each student acts out their term. The student who guesses the term, draws a new card, and acts the new word out.

FLOURISHES:

Divide into groups of four or five students. The teacher calls out a word. Each group cooperatively thinks of a rhyming word for each student in their group, and acts them out so that all of the words relate to each other in some way. If the initial word is *kneel*, the first student pretends to sit in a chair at a table and *feel* his back, the second student pretends to *deal* cards for everyone at the table, the third student pretends to *peel* a banana and lay the peel on the table, and the fourth student eats a *meal* at the table.

Clown White Application

GRADE LEVEL: K-6

MATERIALS: clown white
facial tissues
cotton balls or powder puffs
talcum powder
black or brown eyeliner
red lipstick
cold cream

AREA: classroom

TIME NEEDED: 1 hour

PURPOSE: Although the process rather than the product is usually the most meaningful aspect of creative arts, there are times when the completion of a task is very important. In other words, students really need to see the end result of their efforts. It promotes a sense of accomplishment, and a sincere feeling of self-worth.

When participating in pantomime activities, there may be times, such as a presentation to another class, a PTA program, or an assembly, when facial makeup is especially important. This is where the pantomime face comes in, and the proper application of clown white is a must.

PROCEDURES:

Correct application of clown white described in the steps below ensures that a student will be able to wear it for the duration of the performance.

1. Students apply a thin layer of cold cream to their faces. Have them rub it in so that no excess cream is apparent.

2. Make sure the clown white is at room temperature in order for it to spread onto the face easily. If necessary, hold the clown white container between your hands, or place it near a furnace or heating duct to warm it up.

3. Now have the partners apply the makeup to each other. First use a bit of clown white on the tip of a finger to draw an outline around the area of the face to be covered. The line should start at mid-forehead and should follow the jaw lines along the chin, not under it. Once the oval line has been drawn, fill it in with clown white, making sure the application is even, and not too thick.

4. Once the clown white is evenly covering the face, cover powder puffs or cotton balls with talcum powder and gingerly dab powder over the entire face. When this is done, blow on the entire face to get rid of the excess powder. The talcum powder sets the clown white and allows for tiny scratching if itching occurs.

5. Next comes the application of the *mood symbol* with black eyeliner. Such symbolic drawings could be a teardrop, a sunburst, a heart, or a round circle. Students can decide what kind of mark they wish to have. The drawings should be relatively small and only appear on one side of the face, usually around or below the eye.

6. After the mood symbol, use the black eyeliner and outline the clown white with a black line, making the white stand out more.

7. Last comes the application of the lipstick. Apply the lipstick to the center part of both lips, not the entire mouth.

8. Ask students to wiggle their faces and try to scratch itches that way instead of using their fingernails.

Chapter 5

PUPPETRY

puppetry (pu pe trē) *n.* 1: the art of manipulating puppets 2: a paper sack, some yarn, and imagination 3: a way of bringing a story to life 4: Styrofoam balls gone mad 5: the life and times of Miss Piggy 6: giggles and cloth 7: energy 8: make-believe 9: fun.

Puppetry is an effective learning tool for any classroom. It's easy, it's quick, it can be applied to almost any content area, and, most of all, it's fun. You can be as elaborate or as simple as you want, depending on how you choose to use this creative art in the classroom.

Puppetry can be used in a variety of ways: as a culminating activity to a week long unit, as a way of making a story come alive, to emphasize class rules, and to promote self-esteem. Puppetry works well in combination with creative writing assignments, helps the class celebrate holidays, and gives your students a unique opportunity to master the skills of creating and using puppets.

It is important to consider the age level of your students when deciding which type of puppet you will use. To ask first graders to get out the papier-mâché, sewing machine, sequins, and cloth is setting them up for failure. On the other hand, it will be difficult to get sixth graders involved in paper plates glued to popsicle sticks. Our experience has been that finger puppets, paper plate puppets, and paper bag puppets work best for kindergarten and first grade students. Sock puppets, elaborate paper puppets, Styrofoam container puppets, and plastic bottle puppets work well with higher primary grades. For the older kids, cardboard head puppets, wire puppets, Styrofoam ball puppets, and other, more elaborate, puppets work best.

Puppetry stages can be made of almost anything. Of course an inexpensive, lightweight stage with a curtain is a nice permanent asset to a classroom, but a sheet strung across a corner of a room, a decorated refrigerator box, or two panels of cloth attached to two tension rods, and placed in a door frame are viable alternatives. A stage made of PVC pipe is easy to assemble and inexpensive. For individual puppetry, use a small stage made from a shoe box. With this, the kids can make up their own plays while sitting at their desks. Whatever your preference of stage or puppets, the rewards of using puppetry will far outweigh the time and effort you spend bringing this exciting teaching tool into your class.

There are many many books on puppetry that include puppet scripts for all age groups. Students are also a great source for finding appropriate scripts. Allow them to write their own. Students can work small miracles in retelling favorite stories in their own words. It is imperative that there is some written form of the story before a puppet presentation. If students have a script, whatever form that may take, it makes for a cleaner, less troublesome final product. Students know who speaks when, what to say, and when characters enter or exit the puppet stage. In essence, a script is a blueprint for a successful puppet play. We have included several puppet scripts written by some of our former students that can be used when teaching ecology or environment units.

Using puppetry gives you the possibility of reaching, in a positive and energetic way, every student in your class, regardless of learning style. It opens the doors for self-expression in a safe environment, and empowers your students to make decisions in a very creative way. Puppetry can offer your boys and girls more than what meets the eye; it can touch all of their senses at once. Trust us.

Cardboard Puppet Heads

GRADE LEVEL: 4-6

MATERIALS: cardboard boxes
scissors
materials for decoration (e.g., colored Magic Markers, paints, tissue paper, construction paper)

AREA: stage or large open space

TIME NEEDED: several class periods to construct, one class period to perform

PURPOSE: To practice problem solving skills, to allow group interaction, to design and assemble puppet heads, to develop performance and audience skills.

PROCEDURES:

1. Below are four sample problem-solving scenarios. You may want to write your own situations depending on your topics of study. Scenes A and B require combining the two groups to solve a single problem so the actors in these scenes need to discuss and practice their ideas together.

2. Take each scene, one at a time, and discuss the scene and what the consequences would be in not solving the problems. Do not continue this activity until the students are clear about the purpose of this exercise (problem solving). There must be a solution to each problem.

3. Divide students into proper scene groups. Give them one or two class periods to decide on the solution of the problem. You may want to designate one member of each group to be the recorder, and write down the solutions offered.

4. Each group writes a script for its particular scene. Knowing in advance what each student will be saying alleviates giggles, stuttering, indecision, and blocks of silence. Being prepared also builds confidence in your students, and they tend to take the activity more seriously if it is organized.

5. Once the scripts are written, and the students know the *who, what, when, why*, and *how* of their characters, let them begin making a cardboard box mask of their character.

DIRECTIONS FOR CREATING THE CARDBOARD HEAD:

1. Students should have a cardboard box big enough to fit over their heads.

2. To ensure that the box turns with the student's head, the teacher or the student (depending on the age) should cut a hole in the top of the box (which is really the bottom), so that the top of the student's head can fit into it. This keeps the box firmly placed on the head when in use. Be careful not to cut the hole so large that the box will slip down over the head. Remind students that view holes are essential. These may require help in cutting also.

3. Direct students to read their scenes again, noting the descriptions of their characters. The heads must be decorated to match the character descriptions.

4. Allow the students ample time to complete the construction of the heads. This may take several class periods.

---

5. When all is done, have each group perform for each other, and, perhaps, for other classes or parents. Discuss appropriate behavior, not only for the performers, but for the audience as well.

HINT: When students are rehearsing their scenarios, remind them to project (talk loudly), project (talk even louder), project (let them hear you way in the back of the room), since their voices will be muted somewhat by the boxes, even if a mouth hole is cut.

Scene 1: (4+ students)

You are in the first wave of astronauts who will be settling a newly discovered planet, Zortek, that is already inhabited by natives. The planet is cold and frequently has high winds that obstruct visibility. The two suns are pale in the sky, emitting strong, dangerous gamma rays. The air is composed of nitrogen and carbon dioxide. Snowflakes of sulfuric acid flutter to the ground. Communication among you must be done solely through the space helmet, as to take the helmet off is to die. Your helmet must be self-contained in every way. That is, everything you need to survive must be in, on, around, or connected to your helmet. You speak English, and you do not know the language of the Zortek natives.

The Problem: You must figure out a way to communicate with the Zortekians so that your two cultures can develop a working plan of settlement that will allow for both cultures' survival. It should be made clear why you astronauts need to settle on this particular planet, and why the Zortekians will allow it. In other words, what's in it for both of you?

Scene 2: (4+ students)

You are natives of a faraway planet called Zortek. Astronauts from Earth have just landed and are attempting to develop a working plan of settlement with you. They speak English; you speak Zortekian (your group must invent this language).

Create a family of Zortekians (remembering that no two Zortekians look alike). Your environment is cold with frequent high winds that obstruct visibility. The two suns are pale in the sky, emitting strong dangerous gamma rays. The air is composed of nitrogen and carbon dioxide. Snowflakes of sulfuric acid flutter to the ground. You live in subterranean homes. Remember, though, that this is home and you are designed to live here.

The Problem: You must figure out a way to communicate with the astronauts so that your cultures can develop a plan for settlement that will allow you to live on Zortek together. Make it clear why you Zortekians need to have the astronauts settle on your planet, and why they want to settle here. In other words, what's in it for both cultures?

Scene 3: (8+ students)

You are the characters from the fairy tales, "The Three Little Pigs" and "Goldilocks and the Three Bears." Your scenario will be to combine the two stories into one storyline. The story should be unusual, and the characters can play different roles than in the original stories. For example, Goldilocks could blow the little pigs' houses down.

The Problem: Goldilocks has met and become good friends with Baby Bear. She wants to go visit Baby Bear, but she has forgotten how to get through the woods to the Bears' house. She needs some help. Using the Three Little Pigs and the Big Bad Wolf, figure out how Goldilocks and Baby Bear can get together for a day of play.

Scene 4: (7+ students)

You have lived all of your life on the ocean floor near, on top of, underneath, or inside an old sunken ship. This is home. This is where you feel safe. You are either a marine plant, marine animal or an object that could be found on the ocean floor. Pick what ocean character you would like to be (e.g., whale, treasure chest, shark, octopus, clam, electric eel, fish, or seaweed).

The Problem: An underwater salvage team has discovered long lost treasure in the sunken ship that is your home. It is apparent that before long the salvage team will completely destroy the old ship looking for the treasure chest. How do you stop this from happening?

ACADEMIC VARIATIONS:

Social Studies, Geography, History, Current Events, Science: This can be integrated with the study of practically any unit. In geography, for example, students can create cardboard state puppets, and include facts and figures about each state right on the puppet.

Health: Have students write a script dealing with the hazards of smoking. They could make cardboard box lungs, heart, smoke, and cigarettes. This is also an interesting way to deal with drug related issues.

Language Arts and Reading: Select a favorite story, create a cardboard head puppet for each character, and watch the story come alive.

Creative Writing: Encourage one group to write an original story, and allow another group to act it out with cardboard head puppets. This is a great way to introduce dialogue writing, descriptive words, and original thinking.

Math Story Problems: Once the heads have been created, the cardboard head puppets can continue to be used in the classroom to act out story problems in math, and for the creation of original story problems.

Finger Puppets

GRADE LEVEL: 1-6

MATERIALS: markers
> paste
> cotton balls
> pencil shavings from pencil sharpener
> ribbon
> construction paper
> scissors
> colored yarn

AREA: classroom

TIME NEEDED: 1 hour

PURPOSE: To promote positive self-image, to develop small motor skills, to demonstrate creating a character, to practice speaking and projection, to discuss family and heroes, and to introduce class members through creative expression.

PROCEDURES:

1. Begin this activity with a thorough discussion of *family*. Ask the students to talk about the members of their immediate family, their extended family, and even their pets. Then talk about heroes. What person, apart from their immediate family, do they admire or look up to? Who would they like to change places with for a day if they could? It is important that you model this activity completely. Talk not only about your own family, but when speaking about heroes, be very clear about why that person is a hero to you.

2. Briefly demonstrate how to make a finger puppet. (Pencil shavings make great finger puppet hair. Just put a drop of paste on the tip of your finger and sprinkle on the shavings.)

3. Have students make finger puppets on one hand representing members of their immediate family. On the other hand they are to make one representing their hero, someone they admire and look up to.

4. Have the students sit in a circle and take turns introducing their family and hero to the rest of the class. For older students, teachers may want to limit the speaking time, as fifth and sixth graders sometime get carried away with their introductions, especially when speaking about their heroes.

ACADEMIC VARIATIONS:

Storytelling: Allow students to retell a favorite story by making finger puppet characters. This activity can be done individually or in groups of two or three.

Environmental Education: Give students an appropriate environmental topic such as pollution, overcrowding, noise, and so on. Have them present the issues using their fingers as actors.

Math: For younger children, finger puppets are a marvelous way of making numbers come alive. Each finger is a number with a personality. Students can show how certain fingers can become friends (putting fingers together) to form another number, illustrating the concept of addition.

Music: Teach a song like "This Old Man." Let the students create each man in the song with a different finger, and as they sing the song, they can let that particular man sing his verse.

FLOURISHES:

Take your students, some glue, and lots of puppet making materials, and go outside. Each student will spend some time looking for an object to represent with a finger puppet. This object could be a tree, a rock, a worm, a scrap of paper, a cloud, a leaf, a piece of used chewing gum, or anything else.

Have students sit on the grass, in a group, and describe their puppets in first person without giving away the true identity. The rest of the class will try to guess what the puppet is.

Shadow Puppets

GRADE LEVEL: 1-6

MATERIALS: light colored sheet or cloth
clip light, available at any hardware or auto parts store
long piece of cord or rope
black construction paper or tagboard
scissors
tongue depressors, dowels, straws (optional)
appropriate background music

AREA: corner of classroom

TIME NEEDED: 1 hour

PURPOSE: To develop creative and critical thinking skills regarding the symbolic representation of a storyline, to reinforce sequencing skills, to design characters that illustrate a story or poem.

PROCEDURES:
1. Ask students to select an original story, poem, nursery rhyme, fairy tale, or fable. Divide the students into groups of an appropriate size needed for the particular story or poem.

2. Have students cut out the shape or silhouette of the characters required to tell the story in a meaningful way. Remind students that details do not show up on shadow puppetry, only the outline.

3. Students will then tell their story with one person being the narrator and the others in the group holding up the puppets as needed. Alternately, allow the students to speak their own character lines while holding up their puppets.

4. To make the shadow effect, place the clip light behind the sheet. Allow the students telling the story to stand behind the sheet in front of the light. The closer the student is to the sheet, the clearer the image will be on the sheet. Remind students not to stand right behind the puppet they are holding, or the puppet will get lost in their shadows.

HINT: Puppets tend to be easier to handle if there is a handle on them. A suggestion is to tape or staple either a straw, a small wood dowel, or even a wooden kabob stick to the puppet. Students can move their puppets with more animation with the freedom of movement the sticks provide.

ACADEMIC VARIATIONS:
    Storytelling: Shadow puppetry can be used to make a library book come alive, or to retell a story or folktale.

    Citizenship: This activity is useful for learning class rules, playground rules, and safety rules by role-playing appropriate behavior or discipline situations.

Social Studies: This is a unique way of presenting current events, reviewing milestones in history, studying community helpers, and so on.

Science: This is an excellent method for reviewing life cycles, the water cycle, the effects of erosion on the land, habitats, and environmental issues.

FLOURISHES:

Ask each child or group of children to select a favorite nursery rhyme or fairy tale. Give small sheets of colored cellophane paper to the different groups. Direct each group to cut out characters from the cellophane paper. Now allow each group to tell their story through the use of puppets on the overhead projector. It is a beautiful and colorful way to bring characters to life.

Puppet Plays

The Dangerous Ring

GRADE LEVEL: 5-6

LENGTH OF PLAY: 10-12 minutes

CHARACTERS: 2 children
Narrator
Christy Crab
Sammy Seal
Oscar Octopus
Freddie Fish
Bridget Bird
Storm

SCENE 1: THE BEACH. *(Enter two children.)*

Narrator:
One beautiful summer day, after enjoying time at the beach, a group of environmentally conscious children disposed of their recyclable materials in the proper area. They put their cans in the container labeled "Aluminum" and the plastic six pack rings in the one labeled "Plastics." *(Children throw cans and six pack ring away, then exit.)* Later that evening a storm *(enter Storm)* came up, and a bold gust of wind caught the little six pack ring and carried it out with the ocean tide. *(Storm picks up six pack ring and exits.)*

SCENE 2: MIDDLE OF THE OCEAN.

Narrator:
Two weeks later, in the middle of the ocean a group of friends were playing. *(Enter Freddie Fish, Sammy Seal, Christy Crab, Oscar Octopus.)*

Christy Crab:
Look, look! I found the neatest thing. *(Picks up six pack ring and shows it to the others.)*

Sammy Seal:
Well, what is it, Christy?

Oscar Octopus:
I've seen lots of those before. It's a bracelet made for an octopus, *(sighs)* but it is broken.

Freddie Fish:
(Snobbishly.) No! No! No! It's an exercise device for fish! *(Freddie demonstrates how to use it.)*

Sammy Seal:

(Hesitantly.) I don't know you guys. I think I saw one of those things on old Wise Wally Walrus and he was wearing it on his flippers. In fact, I just heard the other day that he drowned. *(Looks seriously at the rest of the group.)*

Christy Crab:

Oh! You're all wrong! It's a necklace. I know it's so! So don't be silly, Sammy. Hey! As a matter of fact, I think it looks best on you! *(Christy puts the six pack ring around Sammy's neck. Everyone agrees that it looks best on Sammy.) (All exit laughing and hovering around Sammy and his new necklace.)*

SCENE 3: TWO MONTHS LATER IN THE MIDDLE OF THE OCEAN.
(Enter Oscar, Christy, Sammy, Freddie.)

Narrator:

Two months later in their favorite spot in the ocean, all of the animals are playing. Sammy is obviously hurting from the six pack necklace.

Christy Crab:

What is wrong Sammy? Why aren't you playing with us?

Sammy Seal:

This necklace is getting a little tight. I think I'm getting too big for it.
(Enter Bridget Bird.)

Bridget Bird:

Hey! What are you playing huh? Can I play, huh? Can I? Oh, please let me play with you guys. Oh, please! *(Looks at Sammy.)* Oh, what a pretty necklace. Yes, yes, yes, it is pretty, all right. May I see it? Huh? Huh? *(Sammy agrees.)* Oh, yes! How beautiful it is! How I wish I could have one of those. *(Looks at Sammy with admiration.)*

Sammy Seal:

Well, it is getting too small for me, and since you like it so much, I will give it to you. *(Bridget Bird becomes very excited.)*

Narrator:

Sammy tries to take off the necklace but cannot.

Sammy Seal:

Uh, guys, I can't seem to get this thing off. Can someone help me?

Freddie Fish:

Sure Sammy! I'll grab it and pull this way, and you pull the other way. *(Both pull and tumble backwards but are unable to remove the necklace.)*

Oscar Octopus:

Here, let me try. I have more arms to get a better grip on the necklace. *(Oscar tries, but is unsuccessful.)*

Christy Crab:

Oh, move over guys! I guess I always have to get you out of these little messes! *(Christy tries, but cannot remove the ring. The group continues to try to remove the necklace but can't. All exit as they continue trying to remove the ring.)*

SCENE 4: FAVORITE SPOT IN OCEAN.

Narrator:

Another week has passed and the group of friends still haven't been able to remove the necklace to give to Bridget Bird.
(Enter Freddie, Oscar, Sammy, Christy who begin to play.)
(Enter Bridget Bird.)

Bridget Bird:

Oh my gracious! *(Looks at necklace.)* There is that beautiful necklace, again. Can I look at it a little closer?

Sammy Seal:

Yes, but I am still having trouble getting it off. *(Bridget looks at the necklace, and then looks at Sammy, and repeats this action a couple of times.)*

Bridget Bird:

Hey! What kind of joke is this? I'm no bird-brain, born-yesterday, know-nothing, flightless bird, you know. *(Gets a bit huffy.)*

Christy Crab:

What are you talking about, Bridget Bird? I'm really beginning to wonder about you!

Oscar Octopus:

Don't you want the necklace, Bridget Bird?

Bridget Bird:

Yes, but that isn't a necklace.

Freddie Fish:

Oh, but it is, Bridget Bird. Christy told us so, and she always knows about these things.

Bridget Bird:

Nope, nope, nope, not this time. Sillies! That is a human thing. It holds soda cans in it. That is a soda can holder.

Christy Crab:

And how do you know this? Huh? What makes you such a know it all?

Bridget Bird:

I was born at the beach, and I see those things all the time. My mother said they are very dangerous. They can hurt birds because they get all tangled up in our wings. *(Bridget Bird looks at others suspiciously.)* Hey! Pretty sneaky. Yep, yep, yep. That is pretty sneaky all right.

Christy Crab and Sammy Seal:

What is?

Bridget Bird:

Trying to put that thing around my neck to hurt me. *(The others look shocked and then realize that Sammy still cannot get the necklace off, and that it is a danger to him.)*
(All exit.)

SCENE 5: LATER THAT AFTERNOON IN THE OCEAN.

Narrator:

Everyone realizes that they need to get the six pack ring off of Sammy. They all do their best to push and pull, pull and push, to get it off. Later that day, they all get together and try to figure out a way of getting the ring off Sammy's neck.
(Enter all and begin working around Sammy.)

Freddie Fish:

I can't grab hold of it with my fins.

Oscar Octopus:

Well, my tentacles are too big to get a grip on it.

Bridget Bird:

My feathers aren't much help either.

Sammy Seal:

If I could only reach down with my mouth, I could cut it off with my teeth, but I already tried, and I couldn't reach.
(All sigh and look at Christy.)

Christy Crab:

What are you looking at?! I already feel bad enough!

All:

Christy! You can use your claws to cut it off! *(Christy becomes overjoyed.)*

Christy Crab:

(Snobbishly.) Well, it sure took you long enough to think of that. I was just waiting to tell you about it. *(Christy walks toward Sammy proudly.)* Give me room, give me room! *(Christy snaps ring off with her claws.)* There!

Sammy Seal:

Oh, that feels so good! *(Rubs neck.)*

Christy Crab:

I'll just cut up the rest of this thing. That's what should have been done in the first place.
(All cheer and exit.)

Narrator:

It would appear that our story ends here, but not so. Christy, Bridget, Sammy, Oscar and Freddie continued a crusade to make the world's oceans free of six pack rings. Maybe you could join that crusade too.

The End

Today's Tree, Tomorrow's World

GRADE LEVEL: 4-6

LENGTH OF PLAY: 10-12 minutes

CHARACTERS: Narrator
Sue
Jack
Tire
Disposable Diaper
Styrofoam Cup
Black Cloud

SCENE 1: FRONT YARD OF A TYPICAL NEIGHBORHOOD HOUSE.

Narrator:

Sue and Jack are in their front yards talking about their upcoming birthdays.
(Sue enters and begins watering a young tree. Jack enters, drinking from a Styrofoam cup.)

Jack:

Hey, Sue! What are you doing?

Sue:

I'm watering my new tree. I got it for my birthday.

Jack:

(Laughing.) Who would want a tree for a birthday present? My birthday's in a couple of days, and you can be sure I'm getting something better than some dumb old tree! I want robots, airplanes, Nintendo games, and cool stuff like that.
(Jack stomps offstage, muttering under his breath and throws his Styrofoam cup on the ground.)

Sue:

(Yelling after Jack.) Some day you'll understand how important trees are. Just wait, Jack. Just wait. And where do you get off throwing garbage on my lawn? *(Sue picks up cup and exits.)*

SCENE 2: IN JACK'S DREAM.

Narrator:

Later that night, as Jack dreams . . .
(Jack enters, yawns and stretches and appears to be waking up.)

Jack:

Where am I?
(Enter Tire, Disposable Diaper, Styrofoam Cup.)

Tire, Diaper, Cup:

(Singing to the tune of "Lollipop Land" song from *The Wizard of Oz.*)
We represent the garbage you love
The garbage you love,
The garbage you love.
And on behalf of the garbage you love,
We'd like to welcome you
To garbage land.

Jack:

(With disgust.) Wheeewwwww! Who said I love garbage? You guys smell disgusting! This place is gross. And I mean gross. *(Shakes head and holds nose.)*

Styrofoam Cup:

What do you mean? You were the one who threw me on Sue's front lawn 200 years ago. Don't you remember?

Jack:

(Rubs eyes.) No way! This can't be real. I must be dreaming or something. *(Looks around.)* Look at this place! It's a mess. There's garbage everywhere! Gee, you can't even see the houses for all the garbage around here. Where are all the people who live in the houses?

Tire:

People? They had to move out of this dump. They had so much garbage that they couldn't find anyplace to put it. So they just kept piling it up, and piling it up, and pretty soon it took over.

Disposable Diaper:

Yeah, Tire is right. Actually, we think it's a pretty great place to live. Nobody's around bothering us. We pieces of junk and garbage just get to hang around and do nothing. We do have to make room for more garbage all the time, though. I'm afraid that pretty soon there won't be enough room for us here, and we'll have to move on into the junk yard next door.

Jack:

This is too weird for me. I'm getting out of this place. *(Jack tries to run away, but his feet keep getting mucked up in all the garbage. Tire, Diaper and Cup exit, laughing.)*

Narrator:

After much struggling, Jack finally is able to free himself from the heap of garbage that imprisons him. He runs as fast as he can until he comes to a place filled with huge factories and smoke stacks. *(Enter Black Cloud.)*

Jack:

(Coughing and gagging.) What's happening now? I can hardly breathe. Where am I? Look at all this smoke!

Black Cloud:

Hey, Jack! Glad you could join us. We're really lonesome for some human company. All the people around here stay inside the factories. They never come out, because it's so hard for them to breathe.

Jack:

Well, no wonder! This is almost worse than that garbage dump I just escaped. *(Jack coughs and gags again.)* How could anybody let such black, smelly smoke take over everything? What are these factories for, anyway?

Black Cloud:

Oh, we're not just any smoke. Our factories make special medicine for curing scratchy throats and itchy eyes. Everybody uses the stuff. Do you want some?

Jack:

Thanks, but no thanks. I just want to get out of here and get home to Mapletown. *(Black Cloud jumps up and down, laughing.)*

Black Cloud:

You really *are* crazy. This *is* Mapletown, kid.

Jack:

But the last time I saw Mapletown, there were lots of trees and parks and nice houses, not to mention people working and playing outside.

Black Cloud:

Maybe in your dreams! Mapletown hasn't looked like that for years. I should know. I've been around here for at least a hundred years, and it has looked this way for as long as I can remember. From what the old-timers here say, people kept building factories and cars and airplanes, and pretty soon the outside got so full of clouds like me that the people had to stay inside, because they couldn't stand it out here. Personally, I kind of like it.

Jack:

(Puts hand to his head in despair.) What has this world come to? I want things to be the way they used to be ... the way I remember them. I want to go back. There's no place like home ... there's no place like home ... there's no place like home.
(Jack drifts back off to sleep as he keeps repeating the phrase more and more softly.)

SCENE 3: JACK'S BEDROOM.

Narrator:

Asleep once more in his own room, Jack tosses and turns as he prepares to wake up and face whatever the day might bring him. Let's see what happens.
(Jack stirs, then sits up in bed. He opens his eyes wide, jumps out of bed, and moves to the window to see what is outside.)

Jack:

I can't believe it. I must have been dreaming. This is great! Everything is just like it was when I went to bed last night. *(Jack waves at Sue who is outside watering her new tree.)* Hey, Sue! Boy am I ever glad to see you! You won't believe what I've been through. Wait 'til I tell you. I'll be over there in a minute, but first I've got something to do.

Narrator:

Jack's had a tough night, hasn't he? I wonder what he's going to do before he goes down to tell Sue all about his dream? Well, that's for another story, another day. Meanwhile, think about it. What would *you* do?

The End

From *Artstarts*. Copyright © 1994. Teacher Ideas Press, P.O. Box 6633, Englewood, CO 80155-6633.

The Wallet Full of Dreams

GRADE LEVEL: 4-6

LENGTH OF PLAY: 5 minutes

CHARACTERS: Narrator
Monkey
Snake
Toucan
Panther

SCENE 1: THE RAIN FOREST.

Narrator:

Our story takes place in Amazonia, the largest tract of tropical rain forest left in the world. Amazonia is located in South America in the Amazon River Valley. The rain forest is disappearing rapidly due to deforestation—the uncontrolled cutting of trees. As a result, the homes of many animals have been destroyed. But people don't just take things away from the forest, they also leave things behind.
(Enter Monkey whistling. Panther watches from the side.)

Monkey:

Look what I have found. *(Holds a wallet.)* Whoever lost this must be really worried. Mmmm, no identification. *(Turns toward audience.)* If I can't find whose money this is, then I can keep it for myself. There must be a million dollars here! Oh, there are so many things I can buy with it. I know, I'll buy a great big mansion and fill it with monkey bars and banana trees. *(Dream bubble with a picture of a mansion appears about Monkey's head.)*
(Enter Snake who slithers up to Monkey. Dream bubble disappears.)

Snake:

(Sees the wallet.) What isss that?

Monkey:

Oh, hello Snake. Well, you see, I found this wallet with lots of money in it. Look. *(Monkey shows Snake the wallet.)*

Snake:

Did you look for a driver's license?

Monkey:

Yes, but I don't see one. So, if we can't find who the wallet belongs to, then I am going to buy a mansion with the money. *(Dream bubble appears.)* I am going to fill it with monkey bars and banana trees.

Snake:

Ssssuper idea, but I think it would be better spent on a sssilver sssports car. *(Dream bubble with a picture of a car appears above Snake's head.)* I could drive around and visit.... *(Snake and Monkey cease talking and sit dreaming.)*

Toucan:

(Toucan flutters onto stage. Dream bubbles disappear.) Hi guys. What's up? Want to see my new earrings?

Monkey:

Toucan, we found a wallet full of money. There is enough to buy a mansion full of monkey bars and banana trees....

Snake:

Or a sssilver sssports car.

Toucan:

Who does the wallet belong to?

Monkey:

We don't know. There is no driver's license.

Toucan:

What about a major credit card? Visa, American Express, MasterCard?

Monkey:

Nope. There were no credit cards in the wallet either. We can't tell who the money belongs to.

Toucan:

Well then, I could really use some new diamond earrings and necklaces. *(All three have dream bubbles which appear over each of their heads. All sit dreaming.)*
(Enter Panther, who has been watching all of this.)

Toucan:

(Notices Panther. Dream bubbles disappear.) Well hello Panther. Monkey just found what must be a million dollars in a wallet and we can't find any identification.

Panther:

I know. I have been listening to the three of you, and I have an idea of my own. Instead of spending the money on material items for ourselves, we should use it to buy a piece of the rain forest. We could preserve it for generations of monkeys, snakes, toucans, panthers and all other rain forest animals.

Monkey:

I think that is a wonderful idea. If we owned a piece of the rain forest, I could spend all day swinging from the trees.

Snake:

Yesss. And I could ssslither through the forest as fast as I wanted to.

Toucan:

And the forest would be full of beautiful things to enjoy, including me.

Panther:

Are we decided then?

All:

Yes!

Panther:

Then let's make some signs for this lost money. If nobody claims it we will use the money to save our home.

(All animals turn and face audience.)

Narrator:

In the time it took to perform this play, hundreds of trees have been cut down. Unlike trees growing in the United States, the trees in South American rain forests cannot regrow easily. If the rain forests disappear, there will be no more toucans, screeching howler monkeys, or enormous anacondas. The world will never be the same.

The End

Fruitful or Frivolous

GRADE LEVEL: 5-6

LENGTH OF PLAY: 10 minutes

CHARACTERS: Terra
Richard
Yolanda
The King
The Queen
Don
Narrator

SCENE 1: CASTLE SURROUNDED BY TREES AND HILLS AND A VILLAGE. ONSTAGE PUPPET PROPS INCLUDE CHAIR AND BED.

Narrator:

Once upon a nest egg, there was a kingdom, and in this kingdom there lived a king. It was a tradition in this land of opportunity that each child in the kingdom was to receive an endowment of one thousand dollars upon reaching the age of 13. It was the King's ultimate dream that each child, upon receiving this gracious sum of money, would use that gift wisely. This is the story of how four children used their endowment.

(Add banner which says "13th Birthday Banquet" onto castle backdrop.)

(Enter Terra, Richard, Yolanda, and Don. All babble excitedly about the thousand dollar endowment, then exit, except for Terra.)

Terra:

Oh my goodness. One thousand dollars. I know exactly what I'll do with it. I need my planting pot, potter's soil, and my money. I will plant the money and grow a great big money tree. Then I will have millions to share with everybody. *(Goes to back of the puppet stage and works near the trees on the backdrop.)*

(Exit Terra.)

(Enter Richard.)

Richard:

I know exactly what I am going to do with my money. I am going on a shopping spree. I've been watching the department stores for sale signs. I am going to buy an entire new wardrobe, and I can't wait! The money is burning a hole in my pocket already! *(Goes to back of the puppet stage and works near the village section of the backdrop.)*

(Exit Richard.)

(Enter Terra, looking into the pot in which she planted the money.)

Terra:

I am so excited! I'll bet the tree is about to grow itself right out of that pot. I'll have to water it some more, so it can grow up to be a large tree that will be full of thousand dollar bills. *(Looks in pot, sees nothing.)* Oh. *(Sadly.)* It hasn't grown at all. Well, it must be growing a real strong sprout that I can't see so I will water it just a bit more and then come back later on to see how it is doing.

(Exit Terra.)

(Enter Don.)

Don:

I just don't know what to do with this money. It's really very frustrating trying to decide if I should spend it or save it. I just don't know what to do. *(Looks out into space as if in deep concentration.)* I know. I'll put it under my mattress. That's it. I'll hide it in my bed, and that way, no one can find it, and I won't be tempted to spend the money. *(Pretends to hide the money under the bed.)* There! That will do just fine.

(Exit Don.)

(Enter Yolanda.)

Yolanda:

I have been looking forward to this for so long. At first, I wasn't sure what to do with all that money. But then I asked myself, "What is the number one thing that I want?" Clothes? No, what I have is sufficient. Do I want to hide the money? No, then it would do no good at all. Plant it? No, that is a silly idea. Money doesn't grow on trees. No, what I want more than anything is to go away from the castle to a place where I can learn more about the world and the people in it. College. That's where I want to go, and that's what I want to use my money for. So I am going to the bank to deposit the whole amount into a savings account. *(Goes to back of the puppet stage and works near the village section of the backdrop.)*

(Exit Yolanda.)

(Enter Terra.)

Terra:

(Excitedly.) I have said chants. I have performed rituals, I have watered the tree each and every day. Now I am sure it has grown. *(Looks into the pot and sighs.)* What am I going to do? Nothing is happening. *(Exits dejectedly.)*

(Enter Yolanda.)

Yolanda:

Well that was easy. Now all I have to do is wait for it to earn interest. I can't wait to go back to the castle to tell Mom.

(Exit Yolanda.)

(Enter Richard.)

Richard:

What a fulfilling day! I just bought a whole wardrobe. Clothes, clothes, and more clothes! Who could ask for any more clothes than what I have just bought. I have new robes, feathered hats, and riding pants. No one can outdress me now.

(Exit Richard.)

(Enter Terra.)

Terra:

(Chanting.) Money tree ... money tree ... money tree. *(Looks into pot and begins to cry.)*

(Exit Terra.)

SCENE 2: INTERIOR OF THE CASTLE BACKDROP
WHICH INCLUDES A THRONE.

(Enter King and Queen who sit on the throne.)
(Enter Yolanda, Richard, Don, and Terra.)

King:

Each of you received an endowment of one thousand dollars when you turned 13. By now I am sure you have decided what to do with the money. I shall ask each of you what you did with your gift. Terra, what have you done with your money, and was it the best way to use it?

Terra:

Sire, my mom and dad always told me that money didn't grow on trees, but I just never believed them, so I planted my money. I just knew it would grow, and I performed rituals and said chants in order to help it. I waited and watched and waited and watched, but, Sire, nothing happened. It never grew. I probably could have done something better with my money, but then I never would have known that money doesn't grow on trees. So I guess I learned a good lesson. Money really doesn't grow when you plant it. Besides, it gets real wet and soggy if you water it too much.

King:

Richard, do you think you have spent your money wisely?

Richard:

Well, Sire, to be perfectly honest, I guess not. I didn't really think about the future. I was so excited about buying all of these new clothes, but the truth is that these clothes won't fit me when I start growing again and getting older. I guess it would have been wiser to spend just a portion of the money on clothes, and then put the rest away for my future. Yes, that would have been the smart thing to do.

King:

Don, what have you done with your money, and did you use it wisely?

Don:

I put the money under my mattress, Sire. I was afraid I would spend it, so I wanted it out of sight. This way no one could steal it either. I think it would have been better to save it in a bank for my future.

King:

Yolanda, what have you done with your endowment, and was it the best way to use the money?

Yolanda:

Sire, I think what I did was a very good idea. I put it all away in the bank so it could earn some interest. If I had it to do again, I would have bought one small thing for myself, and then saved the rest for my future.

King:

I hope, my children, that all of you have learned something from your mistakes. My greatest desire was that you all would use your endowment wisely. You have made your decisions; some were wise and some were not. Although all of your choices will not always be the very best, you must always remember to learn from them.

The End

Chapter 6

STORYTELLING

storytelling (stōr ē tel ēng) *n.* 1: the act of telling a story 2: magic time 3: oral history 4: "Once upon a time ..." 5: imagination and words 6: Burl Ives and a stool 7: energy 8: vocality 9: fun.

Storytelling comes in many colorful wrappings. It can be a soft voice, a thunderous boom, a trickle of rain. It can be an individual whisper or a group sound effect. It is the time when the mind becomes an artist's palette and brush, drawing one-of-a-kind pictures in each mind, using colors and hues that are unique to each person.

This chapter gives you different activities for using storytelling in your class. But the idea is basically the same. Someone speaks, someone listens. How much easier can it get?

Having had daily access to the public schools we became familiar with a ritual that usually takes place right after lunch. We call this ritual "Magic Time." As we walk the primary halls, and gently tiptoe by the classroom doors, we hear, "... And when he came to the place where the wild things are, they roared their terrible roars ... ," or "I suppose there's another nightmare in my closet, but my bed's not big enough for three ..." or "... As he went along he called 'Caps! Caps for sale! Fifty cents a cap!' But nobody bought any caps that morning. Not even a red one." In the intermediate wing, we may well hear, "If the world was crazy, you know what I'd do? I'd walk on the ocean and swim in my shoe ... ," or "One afternoon, when Fern was sitting on her stool, the oldest sheep walked into the barn and stopped to pay a call on Wilbur...."

That's Magic Time, all right, and it is storytelling. Let your students experience the real thrill of Magic Time. Let them tell the story for a change. It's very simple. Find a comfortable spot on the floor, a big, fluffy pillow might help. Close your eyes, and hug a child next to you. Now, take a deep breath, smile, and listen to a familiar young voice begin, "Once upon a time...."

Collective Story

GRADE LEVEL: 3-6

MATERIALS: tape recorder with blank tape
index cards with the words *Who, What, When, Where, Why* written on them
(one card, one word)

AREA: floor space

TIME NEEDED: 10 minutes

PURPOSE: To strengthen communication skills, to practice sequencing skills, to encourage creative verbal expression, to recognize consequences.

PROCEDURES:

1. Ask the students to sit in a circle on the floor. Place the tape recorder in the middle of the circle.

2. Lead a discussion on storytelling and review the five Ws needed to tell or write a good story (Who, What, When, Where, Why). Place the five cards in the middle of the circle so that all of the students are able to see them. The teacher may want to suggest some storytelling titles that might be fun to do such as: "The Lost Animal," "Fun at the Zoo," "The Mystery Train," "The Cave," "A Trip to the Airport," "Grandmother's House."

3. One person begins telling a story and continues for about 15 seconds. This continues around the circle with each student contributing in some way to the telling of the story. Remind the students that when telling their part of the story, they should look at the cards in the middle of the circle and keep the five Ws of storytelling in mind. Stress continuity and appropriateness. The last person ends the story.

4. At the conclusion, review the five Ws of that story. Make sure that all five were covered.

ACADEMIC VARIATIONS:

Social Studies: When studying different countries and cultures, this is a useful tool for bringing the events to life. For example, tell your class, "Let's pretend we belong to an Eskimo tribe and tell our story of a whale hunt."

Science: After completing an experiment, the students can go through the sequence of predictions and activities of that experiment.

FLOURISHES:

Now it's time for some media arts in the classroom. Give each student a section of a newspaper. Ask them to find one article from that section and read it. Now ask them to find the Who, What, When, Where and Why of that particular article, and list them on a sheet of paper. Now ask students to swap lists. The object is for each student to write a new story using the five Ws on the list they have been given. This exercise covers many skills.

Stories and Sound Effects

GRADE LEVEL: 1-6

MATERIALS: favorite story

AREA: classroom

TIME NEEDED: 10 minutes

PURPOSE: To define character traits, to build self-esteem, to reinforce storytelling skills, to provide a cooperative work situation, to strengthen multicultural awareness and appreciation.

PROCEDURES:

The old-fashioned melodrama format can offer a humorous alternative to encourage students to use their voices in a variety of ways. Here is an example of a well-known story written in melodrama form with the addition of vocal sound effects.

1. Select a reader. The teacher may opt to read instead.

2. Divide the class into a cast of characters (four to six students per character).

3. Explain to the groups that as you read the story, every time you say the name of the character they represent, their group will say, in unison, the prescribed line of dialogue or vocal sound needed and do the action.

4. Give each group a few moments to practice speaking in unison.

5. Reader reads the story aloud.

Most stories, like "The Gingerbread Man," (pp. 109-110) are easily adapted to this melodramatic format. It is also fun for the older students to have the opportunity to present these types of stories to students in the younger grades.

ACADEMIC VARIATIONS:

Creative Writing: Students may create their own original stories, incorporating the vocal sound effects.

Social Studies: During a heritage study, the students can research the folktales and oral traditions of a particular culture, and present them to other classes in this format. This is also an interesting way to discover the legends that describe the geographic wonders of the United States, such as The Paul Bunyan stories.

Science: Write stories using the factual material and combine this information with a fictional situation, incorporating sound effects and movement. This would work well with environmental issues, health situations dealing with drug-related problems, or space study. Also, using sound effects while reading a science textbook can encourage students to pay closer attention to the material.

The Gingerbread Man
Folk Tale

CAST OF CHARACTERS:

Old Woman	puts hands to cheeks and says, "Boy, am I tired."
Gingerbread Man	pumps muscles and says, "I'm a lean, mean running machine."
Old Man	rubs stomach and says, "Is it time to eat yet?"
Horse	neighs like a horse, makes the sound of a galloping horse with hands, and says "Heigh-ho, Silver!"
Lazy Brown Cow	says, "Moo, Moo."
Fox	pretends to hold microphone and sings, "Hit the road, Jack, and don't ya come back no more, no more, no more, no more."
Oven Door	opens arms down and says, "Ummmm" *(long smell sound)*

One day an Old Woman was in the kitchen baking gingerbread cookies. She decided to make some of the dough into a Gingerbread Man. So she gave him a funny little cap with a bright red cherry on top of it and a coat with cloves for buttons. She placed the gingerbread cookies in the oven and after the cookies had baked for awhile, the Old Woman opened the Oven Door and out jumped the Gingerbread Man. He skipped around the room, then ran through the back door singing *(everyone),* "Run, run, run, as fast as you can. You can't catch me. I'm the Gingerbread Man."

The Old Woman ran as fast as she could, but the Gingerbread Man was much too quick. Outside the kitchen door an Old Man was planting some beans in the garden. He looked up and saw the Gingerbread Man and the Old Woman running after him. The Old Man dropped his bag of beans and hoe and began running too. But the Gingerbread Man just laughed and sang *(everyone),* "Run, run, run, as fast as you can. You can't catch me. I'm the Gingerbread Man."

He ran down the road from the house, and cut across a field where a Horse was taking a nap. The Horse woke up in time to see the Gingerbread Man being chased by the Old Woman and the Old Man. The Horse, too, joined the chase, but the Gingerbread Man just laughed and sang *(everyone),* "Run, run, run, as fast as you can. You can't catch me. I'm the Gingerbread Man."

Soon, the Gingerbread Man ran to a pasture where a Lazy Brown Cow was eating some grass. As the Old Woman, the Old Man and the Horse ran by, the Lazy Brown Cow gave chase also, but the Gingerbread Man just laughed and sang *(everyone),* "Run, run, run, as fast as you can. You can't catch me. I'm the Gingerbread Man."

On and on they ran, until they ran into a deep dark forest. The Gingerbread Man became tired and sat down to rest. While resting he spied a sly old Fox who appeared to be asleep. The Gingerbread man quietly sneaked up to the Fox and began to tickle the end of his nose. And as he did he sang *(everyone)*, "Run, run, run, as fast as you can. You can't catch me. I'm the Gingerbread Man."

But as luck would have it, the sly old Fox was only pretending to be asleep, and before you could say "Cooter Brown," he grabbed for the Gingerbread Man, but only managed to get the cherry sitting on top of his hat. This scared the little cookie so badly that he ran away as fast as he could and is probably singing, to this day, *(everyone)*, "Run, run, run, as fast as you can. You can't catch me. I'm the Gingerbread Man."

Sound Effects List

A fun way to make a story come alive is by using sound effects during the telling or acting out of a story. The set up that works best for this kind of addition to storytelling is for the actors to stand around one microphone while the sound effects person or persons stand near another microphone, with a long table in front of them to hold items needed for the sound effects. If you do not have access to microphones, a broom handle stuck in a pail full of sand provides the same effect. This gives the students a feeling of being in a studio and putting on an old radio show. Music stands are useful for holding books or scripts. Common sound effects are:

Fire	crumple cellophane paper.
Thunder	wave large piece of posterboard up and down.
Water	pour water from one container to another.
Gunshot	pop a balloon.
Idea	click light bulb socket chain (found inexpensively at hardware or discount stores).
Chaos	drop bunch of clanky things from one metal pail into another.
Walking	alternate hitting two pieces of wood on a third piece of wood.
Horse	pat thighs in a "gallop-y" sort of way.
Money	drop bottle caps, one at a time, into metal container.
Magic	gently touch small metal wind chimes.
Rustling	crumple up newspaper.
Bees	twang on a rubber band.
Jubilation	play on a kazoo.
Door Closing	slam a large book closed.
Walking in Woods	rustle leaves or cut up paper in a box, break a twig or two.
Lightning	hit two metal rulers or two long pieces of wood together.
Typing	make typing motion with fingers on a tin plate.
Tap Dancing	put two or three thimbles on fingers, tap on tin plate.
Crowd Noise	several people softly mutter "Pencil, Pen, Pencil, Pen" over and over.

FLOURISHES:

To enhance listening skills, bring some sound effects records or tapes to the classroom. Have a class discussion on the different sounds, those immediately familiar to students, and those sounds that take a bit longer to discern. Play a few sounds that are easy to distinguish, and discuss where those sounds might have come from. Then play a mystery sound game. You play a sound on the record. Students write down what they think the sound might be representing, and a different situation in which it could also be used. For example, the sound effect of a sewing machine might also be used for a swarm of bees.

Story Props

GRADE LEVEL: 4-6

MATERIALS: 1 paper lunch sack per student
comb
glove
pencil
glass
matchbox
coat hanger
button
furniture duster
light bulb
fork
quarter
plastic flower
ruler
scissors
Band-Aids
any small object found around the house

AREA: floor space

TIME NEEDED: 20 minutes

PURPOSE: To enliven storytelling, to develop sequencing skills and provide continuity, to provide practice in improvisational speaking, to promote creative expression, to enhance listening skills.

PROCEDURES:

1. Direct the students to sit in a circle on the floor. Place a paper bag with one object in front of each student.

2. Lead a discussion on storytelling with questions like, "What makes a good story?" "Where do story ideas come from?" and "How do writers think of ways to help tell their stories?" Explain that today the class will be telling an original story, using the objects hidden in the paper sacks to help tell the story.

3. Model the activity by beginning a story that is pertinent to the class. For example, "Once upon a time, not long ago, there was a class of fourth graders who were preparing to go on a field trip. They had worked all week long getting ready for the adventure and were very excited. Finally the day came. As they waited in line to get on the bus that would take them to their destination, one of the students said, "Oh no, I have forgotten ..." (at that moment, before finishing the sentence, open up your sack and pull the object out [a comb]). With that object, finish your sentence ... to comb my hair." Add a few words or sentences about combing the hair then freeze the story.

4. Explain that students will each get a turn to tell a part of the story using the prop in the lunch sack in front of them.

5. Students should speak just a few sentences when it is their turn, being careful not to begin the sentence with the words *and*, *uh*, or *er*. Some students may need help in getting started. Remind students that the story should make sense.

ACADEMIC VARIATIONS:

Vocabulary Words: Tell a story using props and vocabulary words combined.

Adjectives: Use this format to review describing words by describing the props in as many ways as you can while telling the story.

Figurative Speech: Tell the story using the props in a figurative sense. For example, a light bulb might indicate a *bright idea*, a piece of yarn might mean you are *all tied up*, a string might indicate someone is *stringing you along*, and a spoon might be used to show you are *fed up*. This is a more difficult variation, and probably works best with older students.

Creative Writing: Put a few props in a box. Have each student select three props and write a story using them. Or select three or four props, and have the entire class write stories using the same props.

Punctuation: As the students tell their story, each student must say the name of the punctuation that will end their sentences. This is a silly way to tell a story, but the older students love it. For example, with a pair of socks as a prop, the story might go, "She was running down the cold snowy street in her socks, period. Suddenly she slipped and fell, muttering, quotation mark, Was that my leg I broke, question mark, quotation mark."

Math Story Problems: Divide the students into groups of four or five. Each group selects three or four props. The group either collectively or individually writes a word problem using the props.

Social Studies: Use props that relate to the history of a time period being studied. The Historic Society frequently has trunks available. Make up a trunk that contains "artifacts" from the Civil War era, the Westward Movement, or archaeological digs, and have the students write a story that revolves around a person or family during the time of the artifacts. With younger children, the props might be hats and tools of various community helpers.

Map Skills: Provide each child or group of children with a road map of a state. As the story unfolds using the props, the students travel through the state on roads of their choice. The students not telling the story must follow on their map so they know what towns, highways, and tourist attractions are near and can be incorporated into their part of the tale.

Science: When studying simple machines, a fun variation is to fill the sacks with simple machines from around the house and school such as pencil sharpeners (inclined plane), bottle openers (lever), egg beaters (wheels), door stops (inclined plane), and retractable clothesline (pulley). Create a story about a student and his adventures with those machines.

FLOURISHES:

Place all objects into a covered box. As the story is being told, push the box around the circle so that when it is time for students to use props, they pull an object out without looking. This time, though, the object cannot be what it actually is. It must be used as something else. For example, a piece of string can become a rope or a snake, or a light bulb can become an earring or a diamond ring.

Story Words

GRADE LEVEL: 3-6

MATERIAL: list of story words
hat

AREA: classroom

TIME NEEDED: 5 minutes

PURPOSE: To enhance creativity in storytelling, to practice sequencing, to demonstrate teamwork, to reinforce listening skills.

PROCEDURES:

1. Divide the class into groups of four or five.

2. Put slips of paper with the following words on them into a hat. Have each group member pick a word.

bean	rose	thirsty	tornado
tree	disappear	mad	tide
beaver	volcano	heat	desert
plane	run	hurricane	sugar
love	tattle	beach	empty
brother	shadow	light	sing
winter	tale	weep	ocean
winner	surprise	odor	monster
mistake	buddy	mother	fear
eagle	holler	laughter	quick
gone	sister	moon	friend
tears	baby	dinosaur	sorry
building	error		

3. Now each group must combine their words and write a collective poem or a story using all of the new words.

4. As each group reads the poems or stories, the rest of the groups must try to guess which words are from the word list.

ACADEMIC VARIATIONS:

Language Arts: Review of adjectives, verbs, adverbs, nouns.

Social Studies or Science: Make a list of the appropriate vocabulary words to use.

FLOURISHES:

Using this same format, ask each group to select five words. Have each group draw a composite picture representing the five words. Remind each group that the picture must be logical and complete, not five separate pictures or drawings. When all groups have finished, see if each group can locate the words selected for the drawings of the other groups.

Chapter 7

VISUAL ARTS

visual (vizh wul) *adj.* 1: ocular 2: pertaining to sight.

arts (ärts) *n.* 1: magic 2: the conscious use of skill and imagination.

visual arts (vizh wul ärts) *n.* 1: God's rainbow 2: a lesson plan for the hands and eyes 3: music without notes 4: finger paints and bubblegum 5: Mother's Day cards 6: soap carvings and sequins 7: purple and lime green smiles 8: energy 9: texture 10: fun.

Like all of the other art forms, visual arts appeals to the soul. It is the ultimate hand-eye coordination and has a vital place in the classroom.

But asking the students to illustrate the story they have just read or draw how they feel are not the only ways to use visual arts. While these are certainly credible approaches, they are by no means the only way to get the kids to use their crayons, markers, tempera paints, finger paints, and pencils. Visual arts is anything the eye or imagination sees and then asks the hand to do. It is molding, shaping, building, spreading, pasting, tearing, forming, coloring, blending, dyeing, weaving, and a thousand other things.

Your school art specialists are the backbone of the visual art experience in your school so use these talented people to the fullest. When you are studying a culture in social studies, ask the specialists about that culture's art customs. If you are doing a play, talk to the specialist about the sets and scenery. Have the art specialists come in and discuss plants from which we get natural dyes and the colors that come from certain plants. Ask them to tell your class about prehistoric cave drawings. Your art specialists can give you great suggestions on the making of puppets.

There is also a wealth of talent in your community. Ask local painters, potters, weavers, and other artists to come into your classroom and demonstrate different visual arts techniques. Use every means available to bring the glory of color, texture, and form to your students.

Whatever the medium, whether it's finger paints, tear art, soap sculpture, or collage, the object is to give your students the chance to explore the magical, renewing world of visual arts. Most kids have an eye for it. Just give them encouragement, freedom, and permission to experiment.

Art/Story/Music

GRADE LEVEL: 2-6

MATERIALS: long sheet of light colored butcher paper
markers or crayons
tape player
a selection of classical, environmental, or soft piano music

AREA: open floor space

TIME NEEDED: 20 minutes

PURPOSE: To express original ideas through pictures, to infer the meaning of a picture, to work cooperatively, to recognize individual space, to reinforce sequencing skills.

PROCEDURES:

1. Roll out a long piece of light colored butcher paper. Place a crayon or marker for each child along the edge of the butcher paper. Ask students to seat themselves around the edge of the paper behind a crayon or marker. It is best if only 12 or 13 children sit around each sheet of paper, and if the students don't sit on the paper or jump over it.

2. Begin playing quiet, appropriate music that fits the mood of the selected theme of the art project.

3. Begin talking about a theme, like transportation and all of the different ways people through history have gotten from one place to another.

4. When initial discussion is complete, each student starts drawing one mode of transportation. When you clap your hands, the students stop drawing. Allow 10-15 seconds between claps. Now the students take their crayon or marker and move to the picture to the right, and finish what has been started, or if the drawing is complete, add something else that relates to the picture at hand. For example, if the first drawing is a riverboat, other students might draw the riverbank, trees hanging down into the water, fish, people on the riverboat, the paddle wheel, and so on.

5. Continue until the students work themselves back to their beginning place, where they look at their original picture and add anything they wish.

6. Students will title their drawing, and then either:

   Tell about their picture.
   Write a story about their picture.
   Act out their title and story.
   Get in groups and act out one story.
   Describe the title through movement.
   Write a song or poem about the picture.

HINT: It is very important at the outset to discuss appropriate guidelines when doing this activity. Students should not be allowed to write words on any part of the drawings, nor draw over what someone else has drawn. Discourage scribbling or crossing out.

ACADEMIC VARIATIONS:

Science: Discuss a concept in science such as machines and their uses. Set up a scenario for a pretend machine and a pretend function, for example, an *automatic eraser duster*. Students will create the machine as they "draw to the right." When they get back to their original starting point, allow them to retitle their machine if the machine in front of them looks like something else. With older students, they can label the parts of their simple machine.

Reading: Read a fairy tale or well-known story. Ask students to draw the characters, settings, important objects, and important scenes as you read the story.

Emotions: Read a story. As you come to an emotion in the story, ask students to draw that emotion in an abstract way. This is a great way to review geometric shapes.

Social Studies: When reviewing a historical period, have students draw what the houses were like in those days, how the people dressed, the modes of transportation, and important historic events.

Environment: Allow students to share beautiful places they have traveled to. Use this activity to allow students to draw a montage of things that are beautiful in nature. Remind the students that if someone begins drawing a mountain, then the entire picture must be on the theme of mountains.

FLOURISHES:

Take a field trip and remind the class to remember what they see and do, or even keep a journal of the trip. Once the trip is completed, make a list of all of the events of the trip. Let students select an event, and illustrate it through their own visual art method.

Now take the students to an open space, and ask them to line up their artwork according to the sequence of events.

Back Art

GRADE LEVEL: 4-6

MATERIALS: blank paper
                masking tape
                pencils or crayons
                appropriate music

AREA: classroom

TIME NEEDED: 20 minutes

PURPOSE: To develop self-concept, to show positive communication. This exercise is a good culminating activity to a positive situation such as a successful week at school, a self-image lesson, or a teamwork unit.

PROCEDURES:

1. Have students tape a blank piece of paper on their backs.

2. Begin playing appropriate music, and ask the students to walk around the room and write one positive comment on the backs of the other students, emphasizing the necessity for appropriate language and positive comments. You monitor the comments.

3. When the students have had the opportunity to write on each other's backs, direct them to take the paper off of their own backs, fold it up, and not look at it until bedtime that evening.

4. Instead of writing, each student may wish to draw a positive picture on the blank paper. A follow-up discussion may be necessary the next day.

ACADEMIC VARIATIONS:

Science: When studying space, have each student write a different word from the unit on a piece of paper and tape it to their backs. Play the theme from *Star Wars*, and have the class walk around the room, writing everything they know about the words that are on each other's backs.

FLOURISHES:

Ask students to make a list of all the adjectives that were on their papers after this exercise. Direct students to paint an abstract of how they are viewed by other people, using finger paints or watercolors to depict the mood or tone of the words on their list. If this self-esteem activity is done correctly, there should be no dark colors on the abstract painting. Students may want to title their drawing when they have finished. This is a nice conclusion to an important lesson.

Bag It

GRADE LEVEL: 2-6

MATERIALS: One plastic bag for each student containing the following items:

rubber bands	plastic straw
paper clips	popsicle stick
brad	wad of modeling clay
tongue depressor	cotton balls
tacks	clothespin
pipe cleaners	small scrap of material
string	

AREA: classroom

TIME NEEDED: 15 minutes

PURPOSE: To comprehend the meaning of sentences, to think creatively and to provide expression for compositions, to draw conclusions, to improve hand-eye coordination, to create an object.

PROCEDURES:

1. Give each student a plastic bag containing the above items.

2. Ask students to take the objects out of the bag and place them in front of them.

3. Discuss the objects and their common uses in daily life. Then explain that the objects will be used in a different way to make sculptures that illustrate sentences you are going to read.

4. Direct students to use some of the objects to make a sculpture that answers the question, "Isn't it beautiful? I just bought it today." Other suggested sentences include:

   "I love that smell. What is it?"
   "Your Dad needs one of these at the office."
   "I'll show you what's been making all that noise."
   "Look what I found! It's so small!"
   "Please, find me something that will help me see better."
   "Oh, I found it on the sidewalk."
   "But I don't want it."
   "Whew! It smells awful."
   "It's the prettiest thing I have ever seen."
   "What do you think is in the package under the tree?"
   "I'll trade you this for that marble."
   "I just reached in the hole and pulled it out."

5. Allow students time to share their creations after each sentence. Remind them to carefully replace the objects in the bags when the activity is over, so that they will last a long time.

ACADEMIC VARIATIONS:

Reading: After reading a story, check comprehension by asking questions that can be answered through this activity. For example, "What did the rabbit use to trick the fox?"

Sponge Activity: Give students an oral question from a chapter in social studies, science, health, or a math story problem. Students, instead of answering verbally, will sculpt the answer.

FLOURISHES:

To use this activity as a creative writing catalyst, allow students to pair off and sculpt one object between them. When all of the objects from each pair of students are placed on a table, ask the students to select one or several to write a story about. It may be fantasy, science fiction, a poem, or whatever their imagination suggests. You will be amazed.

Blow Art

GRADE LEVEL: 2-6

MATERIALS: white art paper
glue
plastic straws cut into 3 or 4 inch lengths
newspapers
tempera paint
small paper cups
black permanent markers
colored construction paper

AREA: classroom

TIME NEEDED: 1 hour

PURPOSE: To use colors as illustrations of a piece of written work, to combine two art disciplines, to work independently, to demonstrate following directions, to create a poem.

PROCEDURES:

1. Students will review or be introduced to writing cinquain poems. Demonstrate by writing one or two cinquains on the board so that your class can see the format. Remind them that writing a cinquain is as follows:

line 1	one word	(a title)
line 2	two words	(describes the title)
line 3	three words	(tells an action)
line 4	four words	(tells a feeling)
line 5	one word	(synonym for line 1)

   Examples:

Balloon	Emotions
Round, yellow	Subtle, alive
Floating in air	Piercing the heart
To color the sky	To let souls breathe
Circle	Feelings

2. Students will decide on a topic, or the teacher will provide a single topic for all of the students. Using dark markers or crayons, students write cinquains about their topic on a piece of white art paper. Have students blow tempera paints, a drop at a time, across the art paper using the short straws, creating interesting patterns on the paper surface. Remind students that if the tempera paint is too thick and will not run, to put some paint into a paper cup and add a tiny bit of water. Provide lots of newspapers to work on, as this activity is usually quite messy.

3. Once the tempera has dried, students mat their finished product with a piece of construction paper to give it a framed effect.

ACADEMIC VARIATIONS:

Social Studies: Have older students write the name of a well-known historical figure on a slip of paper. Place all of the slips in a hat and have the students select a name, making sure they do not pick the name that they wrote. Have students write a cinquain about that person. For example, a cinquain about Ben Franklin might look like this:

Inventor
smart, stretching
playing with kites
touching the night energy
Ben

Students write the cinquain onto art paper and illustrate it through blow art in a way that will be appropriate to the subject.

Once the projects have been completed, students will go to the front of the class, read their cinquains, then present that piece of artwork to the person who had written the name in the first place.

Environmental Education, Reading, Health, Science: This same format can be used successfully for most subject areas. We believe that the give-away at the end of the experience is the most valuable aspect of the entire activity.

FLOURISHES:

Have students write a cinquain about one or both of their grandparents. Then have them illustrate the creative writing with blow art, frame it with matte board or construction paper, and then invite their grandparents to come and spend the day with the class where they can hear the poems and receive the artwork. What a nice way to say, "I love you."

Class Flag

GRADE LEVEL: 3-6

MATERIALS: felt
large piece of white cotton backing
embroidery thread and needles
fabric glue
fabric scraps

AREA: classroom

TIME NEEDED: several class periods

PURPOSE: To create a positive self-image, to emphasize individual differences, to create a unique class emblem, to instill a sense of community.

PROCEDURES:
1. Lead the class in a discussion of the importance of self-worth and individual differences. At the end of the discussion, explain to the class that they will be making a class flag that will hang in the room for the entire school year. Each student will be responsible for making a section of the flag.

2. Give students time to think about how they will represent themselves as individuals. If students have trouble deciding, you may want to suggest ideas such as:

   What are their strengths?
   What do they want to contribute to the class for the upcoming school year?
   What do they like best about themselves?
   What are their personal goals for the year?

3. Ask students to use a piece of blank paper to draw their design before cutting, pasting, sewing, or drawing on the pieces of felt.

4. Once the designs have been planned, distribute felt squares to each of the students. Place the rest of the materials, such as ribbon, sequins, cotton balls, leather strips, and glitter where they will be easily accessible. Play soft instrumental music and allow the students to make their own flag piece.

5. When all of the sections have been completed (several class periods), allow students to attach their design square onto the large white heavy cotton piece that will be used as the flag backing. Felt squares stay on more securely if sewn on, but cloth glue will suffice.

ACADEMIC VARIATIONS:
   Creative Writing: Use the flag as a stimulus for poetry, cinquains, short stories, or a composite story.

Social Studies: Divide the class into pairs. Each pair will select a country, do research on that particular country's flag, make the flag, and attach it to a larger world flag. Or use individual squares to reflect different aspects and events of a time period in history.

Reading: This can be an interesting addition to, or substitute for, written book reports. Each student makes a square for the reading flag which shows their favorite part of the book or the traits of their favorite character.

FLOURISHES:

With the support of your principal, work with other classes to make a school flag. Each class in the school creates its own unique piece of the flag. Gather all the sections, sew them all together onto a sturdy cloth background, and hoist it up the flagpole in front of the school.

Comportrait

GRADE LEVEL: 1-6

MATERIALS: 1 large piece of light colored butcher paper per group
crayons and markers
tape

AREA: floor space

TIME NEEDED: 45 minutes

PURPOSE: To develop self-esteem, to learn more about each other, to practice cooperative learning.

PROCEDURES:

1. Lead a class discussion on the value of individual differences.

2. Divide the students into groups of five or six, making sure that best friends are not grouped together.

3. Tell the groups that they are to draw an imaginary person that is a composite of the best features of each of the members of the group.

4. You might have the class brainstorm as many physical traits, personality characteristics, or individual interests as they can think of that apply to different students in the class. For example, some members of the class may be fast runners, hence they may want to draw the feet for their group's picture. Other students may have pretty hair or a nice smile. Still others may be funny or extra friendly. The groups individually discuss and draw their comportraits.

5. When the drawings are finished and hung up for everyone to see, allow time for the groups to share their comportraits and explain why things were drawn the way they were. Students should be allowed to speak about their own contributions to the comportrait.

ACADEMIC VARIATIONS:

Social Studies: When studying cultures and customs, create comportraits of the best characteristics of those cultures.

Science: During an environmental study, allow the students to create imaginary comportrait creatures who have adapted to thrive in a given environment, such as an oil slick, inner city sewer, or a burned out rain forest. While studying space, the students may develop creatures who could live on the different planets or stars. Simple to complex machines can also be created this way, as can new modes of transportation or housing for the future.

FLOURISHES:

Divide the students into groups. Give each group a number (e.g., 14). They must draw a picture of a person composed of different math equations that use addition, subtraction, multiplication, or division to make the number 14.

Listen and Draw

GRADE LEVEL: 3-6

MATERIALS: drawing paper or newsprint
crayons

AREA: classroom

TIME NEEDED: 30 minutes

PURPOSE: To strengthen listening skills, to practice following directions.

PROCEDURES:

1. Give each student a crayon and a piece of drawing paper or newsprint, and ask them to find a comfortable space on the floor facing the teacher.

2. Explain to students that you will tell them what to draw on their paper and where to draw it. Tell students that they must listen attentively to the directions, as you will not repeat them once you have given them. They are to look only at their paper and try to do exactly as you instruct. The object is to see if they can draw a picture exactly like yours by just listening.

   See page 129 for an example of a picture that you will need to draw ahead of time.

3. Give the students the following directions regarding the first drawing:

   a. Lay your paper horizontally rather than vertically.

   b. Draw as big a circle as you can on the page.

   c. In the middle of the circle draw a dot.

   d. Draw a straight line from the top of the circle, through the dot, to the bottom of the circle.

   e. Draw a straight line from the left side of the circle, through the dot to the right side of the circle.

   f. In the bottom right-hand section of the circle, draw three flowers in a row. Make sure that each flower has a stem and eight petals.

   g. In the top right-hand section of the circle, draw a big four.

   h. In the top left-hand section of the circle, draw a big smiley face with two black eyes and a smile.

   i. In the bottom left-hand section of the circle, draw a big *B*.

   j. In the top loop of the *B* draw a number seven. In the bottom loop of the *B* draw a number eight.

4. Upon completion of this activity, allow the students to show their drawings to the rest of the class and compare their drawings with yours and those of the other class members.

From *Artstarts*. Copyright © 1994. Teacher Ideas Press, P.O. Box 6633, Englewood, CO 80155-6633.

ACADEMIC VARIATIONS:

Since this is basically an activity for listening and following directions, it can be integrated into any other content areas by varying the drawings to fit a certain subject.

Math: Instead of telling students which number to draw, give them a math problem, and have them draw the answer. This is also a fun way to review geometric shapes or concepts.

Social Studies or Science: This activity could be used to review concepts or strengthen and review vocabulary. For example, draw a horizontal rectangle. In the top right-hand corner, write the name of the rock that the Pilgrims landed on vertically, draw in the lower corner the country they left, and write or illustrate two things that occurred on the voyage to the New World.

FLOURISHES:

Divide kids into pairs. Give each student a piece of paper and a crayon, and ask each pair to find a comfortable space on the floor and sit back to back. Have each student draw something on their paper, reminding them to keep the objects simple enough that another person could draw them. Now have the partners describe their drawings while the other tries to duplicate it by listening to the directions. Be sure to let each student get a chance to draw as well as describe.

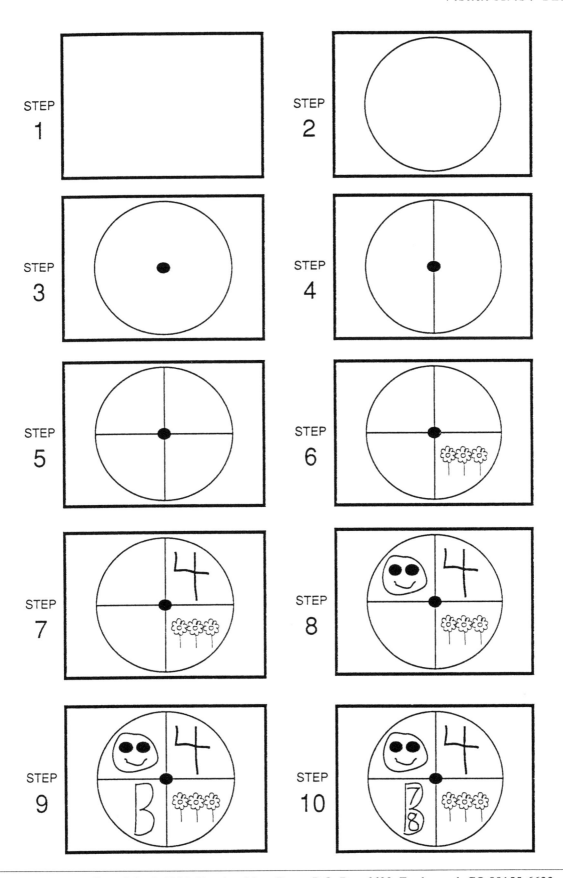

Mask Making

GRADE LEVEL: 3-6

MATERIALS: adhesive bandaging
plastic margarine containers
petroleum jelly
scissors
tempera paint
1 towel per student
1 pillow per student
1 old T-shirt or smock per student

AREA: floor space

TIME NEEDED: 2 class periods

PURPOSE: To work with a partner in a trusting way, to understand the definition of masks, to create a mask, to demonstrate creative expression.

PROCEDURES:

1. Before the mask-making begins, ask students to take rolls of fast-drying adhesive bandaging, which can be purchased at most medical supply stores, and cut them into one-inch strips. Most masks require 42-45 strips of bandaging.

2. Have the students wear an old T-shirt, bring an old pillow to rest their heads on, and use an old towel to cover their clothes while the masking material is being applied to their faces. Students work in pairs and take turns applying the bandage strips to each other's faces.

3. Before application, students should cover the entire surface of their faces with a liberal amount of petroleum jelly, especially over the eyebrows, eyelashes, and temple areas where there are tiny hairs. This will alleviate painful pulling when the masks are removed from the face.

4. Give students the choice of doing a whole mask, with eyes and mouth covered, a mask with eyes uncovered, a mask with mouth uncovered, and a mask with both eyes and mouth uncovered. For those students who wish not to have material such as bandaging on their faces, an alternative is to make a mask of one of their hands.

5. When applying the masking material, each strip of adhesive should be dipped into a bowl of water to soften it. Be sure to remove excess water before applying the strip to the face.

6. Begin the process by applying strips to the forehead first, remembering to criss-cross to ensure strength. After the forehead has been covered with layers of bandage strips, begin criss-crossing the strips around and down the temples, then on down the jaw line, and around the front of the chin. Don't apply underneath the chin, as it is difficult to remove the hardened mask without that area breaking.

7. Continue applying until the facial outline has been completed. Now fill in the rest of the face, criss-crossing over one closed eye first, then another, then the cheeks, the bridge of the nose, above the chin, the mouth, and finally above the nose, making sure not to cover the nostrils.

8. The material will begin to harden immediately, and the entire mask should be ready to be removed about three minutes after the final strip has been applied.

9. Once the mask has hardened, have students begin wiggling their faces to loosen the mask, and get it to pop free of the mouth and chin. Then gently begin lifting the mask away from the face.

10. Let the masks dry for a day or two, then decorate them with tempera paint and objects that the students might want to add.

HINT: When working with students younger than 4th grade, you may want to enlist parents to come in and help with this activity.

ACADEMIC VARIATIONS:

Social Studies: Once the masks are completed, but before you decorate them, go to the library and do some research on masks of different cultures around the world. Students may want to decorate their own masks based on a certain culture. A written or oral report about the culture would be a nice addition to this activity.

Creative Writing: Let students get into groups of four or five, write an original folk tale about their masks, and present it in a puppet presentation.

FLOURISHES:

Have students decorate their masks as they really see themselves. In other words, as lifelike as possible. Then have students make a stuffed body that they can attach to the mask. Place the dummies in desks for Open House, make them into a bulletin board that stresses individual differences, or place them around the room as interesting conversation starters.

Mirror Art

GRADE LEVEL: 3-6

MATERIALS: 1 mirror per child
drawing paper
pencil

AREA: desk

TIME NEEDED: 20 minutes

PURPOSE: To practice observing details, to practice creative expression through visual arts, to develop a sense of self, to imitate what is being seen, to work independently.

PROCEDURES:

1. This activity should begin with a discussion of differences. Show your class pictures of animals that seem to be the same, like cows. Then show other pictures demonstrating the differences among cows. The discussion should eventually lead to differences among the members of the class. Who is blond? Who has short hair? Who wears glasses? Who has missing teeth?

2. Instruct the students to look at themselves in the mirror, and, using a soft lead pencil, draw what they see. Ask them to notice specific details about themselves. Do they have blue eyes? Do they have long eyelashes? Do their ears stick out? Are their faces covered with freckles? Do they have any characteristic scars?

3. Explain that if they do notice a feature that is unique, such as those mentioned above, they are to exaggerate that feature in their drawing; that is, make that feature larger than it really is. You model this with your own drawing. Remind students not to erase too much. Perfection is not the goal.

4. Have students color their drawing or leave it in pencil as they choose.

5. A discussion regarding strong physical features, likenesses, differences, and the importance of each should conclude this activity.

ACADEMIC VARIATIONS:

Reading: Direct students to read a children's story, define the characters, and then illustrate those characters by looking in the mirror, making facial expressions that best describes those characters, and drawing what they see.

FLOURISHES:

For the older students, drawing original comic strips is a lot of fun. Give students a topic and have them create a four or five cell comic strip giving information concerning the topic. Have them illustrate the strip by using their own facial expressions as they act out the emotions in the comic cells.

A variation is to have the students create a comic strip describing themselves or interesting events in their lives. Again, they would use mirror art to illustrate the strip.

Peepboxes

GRADE LEVEL: 2-6

MATERIALS: 1 shoe box and lid per student
several cardboard boxes (optional)
colored cellophane paper
glue
scissors
cotton balls
stick-on stars
construction paper
string
pipe cleaners
fabric pieces

AREA: classroom

TIME NEEDED: 1 hour

PURPOSE: To develop self-expression, to build a model to scale, to strengthen creative imagination, to discuss setting mood, to review material by creating scenes.

PROCEDURES:

1. Give each student a shoe box with a lid. Depending on their age, have them use scissors to cut out a square hole in the middle of the lid and a peephole in one end of the box.

2. If the scene the student is going to create is warm (e.g., daytime, summer, beach, and so on), suggest that the student tape or paste a piece of yellow, red, or orange cellophane paper over each hole. If the scene is going to be cool, suggest the student tape or paste a piece of blue, green, or purple cellophane over each hole. Discuss how the different colors reflect different moods.

3. Have students make a three-dimensional scene inside the shoe box. Objects can be attached to, glued on, propped up, hung down, silhouetted, or drawn anywhere inside the box or underneath the lid. Give the students as many kinds of material to choose from as possible.

4. When the scene is completed, and the lid is attached, the viewer looks at the scene through the peephole.

ACADEMIC VARIATIONS:

This art activity can fit into any subject you teach.

Social Studies: Create scenes from outer space colonies, different countries, the community, the home, or during historical events. Imagine being at an archaeological dig, show a museum of artifacts from the Anasazi culture.

Science and Environmental Education: Create scenes that show solutions to pollution problems, the effects of different types of light and environments on plant or animal growth, and different types of weather systems. Use half the box to show how the habitat could change as a result of an ice age, the greenhouse effect, or a volcanic eruption.

FLOURISHES:

Get several large boxes. Divide your kids into groups of four, and give each group a topic (e.g., planets, deserts, oceans, cities, animal habitats or jungles) and lots of materials for making large peepboxes. These will require larger peepholes and more than one light source in the lid. Give each group ample time to research what needs to be included in their peepbox.

As a variation, give each group the same topic and use the activity as a discussion of comparisons.

Story Sculpture
The Oobligoodle

GRADE LEVEL: 2-6

MATERIALS: 5 paper sacks containing:

1 pair scissors	pipe cleaners
1 bottle glue	feathers
string	beads
construction paper	tongue depressors
tissue paper	paper plates
cotton balls	paper cups

AREA: classroom

TIME NEEDED: 40 minutes

PURPOSE: To enhance listening skills, to promote creative expression, to apply cooperative learning skills, to design a creature using nonverbal communication skills, to strengthen imagination.

PROCEDURES:
1. Fill five paper sacks with the above materials, making sure to put a different assortment into each sack. Divide the students into five groups. Ask each group to sit on the floor away from other groups. Place a closed sack in the middle of each group. Tell students not to look inside the sacks.

2. Explain that you are going to tell them a story. Remind them that they need to listen very carefully to the story because remembering details of the story will come in handy later on.

3. Play some weird or scary sounding music and ask the kids to get into a comfortable position as you read the story slowly, and with great expression. ("The Oobligoodle" is on p. 136.)

4. Direct students to open the sacks in front of them. Without communicating verbally, the students use the materials inside the sack to make their own version of the Oobligoodle. Be sure to monitor their communications methods, as it is vital that they not speak when doing this activity. Continue playing appropriate music.

5. When the Oobligoodle creatures have been made, have each group select a spokesperson to explain that group's creature and why it was made the way it was.

6. If time permits, discuss the ways the students were communicating. What was difficult about not speaking? What kind of communication did each group use? Why did it work? Ask the school librarian for permission to display the Oobligoodles in the Halloween section of the library or near the Fairy Tale books.

The Oobligoodle

by Martha Brady

Far, far away, on the other side of the tallest mountain, carefully hidden beneath the tall, skeletal trees, and nestled among huge boulders, there lies a small village. It is winter, and there is no movement, except for the gentle smoke rising above the tops of the thatched roofs. The wind blows in long whispers and brings with it the rustling sounds of tree branches touching and long dead leaves dancing. Stretched long and narrow beside the village is a deep lake covered with the first layer of winter's ice. The shimmering, icy cover creaks and groans as it settles. The fish beneath it dream of wiggly worms and gnats and plump dragonflies.

Slowly, night falls and paints shadows across the village. There are no lights in the houses and there is no sleep among its dwellers. There is only the watching of the clock ... tick ... tock ... tick ... tock ... and the waiting ... waiting ... waiting for morning.

As the morning sun pulls itself up over the largest mountain and spills its warmth onto the waiting village below, something stirs beneath the icy surface of the lake. The stir becomes a rumble. The rumble becomes a clamor. The clamor becomes the crashing, heaving, spitting, and growling sound of *The Oobligoodle*. The Oobligoodle is awake and he is hungry!

He pushes himself up from his icy nest and surges with uncontrolled power to the land. He hasn't eaten enough for the long winter months ahead, and his terrible, ravenous hunger propels him toward the tiny village.

Tramping onward, the Oobligoodle eats everything in sight: an apple tree, a family of squirrels, bushes, birds, three cats, a light pole. As he nears the frightened village, his appetite increases. He eats a bread truck, the golden arches of a McDonald's, and a milkman—breaking, snapping, crunching, ripping, shoveling, swallowing. He engulfs a double-wide mobile home, pausing only to spit out the shag carpet caught between his teeth; he devours a tourist information booth, a billboard sign advertising a monster truck competition, and finally a wad of chewing gum. Then he stops. He is full. He can eat nothing more.

The Oobligoodle becomes drowsy now, heavy, and satiated. He lumbers slowly back to the lake, back to the freezing, hidden cavern that is his home. With eyes half-closed, and the rattled sounds of deep breathing coming from inside his huge frame, the Oobligoodle flings himself onto the hard cover of the frozen water, breaking it into more jagged sections. Quickly he sinks, down, down, down ... to bed ... to sleep ... until he has to eat, again.

ACADEMIC VARIATIONS:

Creative Writing: Read the above story, but leave out the ending, and let students write their own. Or let each group think of their own creature and write about it.

Adjectives or Adverbs: Have each group make a list of all of the descriptive words they can remember from this story, or list other descriptive words that could have been used to describe the creature.

Map Skills: Have each group decide where, on the playground, the icy lake and Oobligoodle are, then make a map that leads to the spot.

Science: Direct a discussion of what kinds of animals live under water, or in freezing cold, or both on land and under water. How have these animals adapted to their habitats?

Reading: Ask the librarian to spend some time with your class researching stories similar to "The Oobligoodle." Allow the students to share those books, and make comparisons.

Media Arts: Let each group make a filmstrip of their story, using acetate strips, and transparency markers (markers that work on this type of material).

Visual Arts: Allow the class to create a tear art mural of the Oobligoodle. Or have students make their own book cover to illustrate their original stories.

FLOURISHES:

Direct groups to use their Oobligoodle as the main character for a puppet story, but give them extra materials (paper plates, plastic milk cartons, paper sacks, socks) to create additional characters. This could take several days.

Chapter 8

MEDIA ARTS

media (mē dē a) *n.* 1: modes of expression
or communication.
arts (ärts) *n.* 1: the conscious use of skill and
imagination.
media arts (mē dē a ärts) *n.* 1: transmitting
an idea in a magical way 2: acetate and
old lace 3: eat your heart out, Allen Funt
4: film at eleven 5: lights, camera, action
6: energy 7: fun.

The use of media arts in the curriculum is becoming more popular, as the availability of video cameras in the classrooms has increased. Media arts is a great area in which to work, because it has a modern feel, because it incites real interest in today's technologically aware children, and because it is fun. Students love the responsibility involved in using media arts, and because they are dealing with more costly equipment they treat cameras and acetate strips for filmstrip making with respect.

Working in this medium requires organization, effort, time, and a little camera knowledge. The time factor keeps many teachers from bringing a camera into their room. The equipment is often in high demand, an equipment problem can slow things up enormously, and then there's the excitement cameras cause in your students, which can lead to hyped up, distracted students all day.

Some teachers just haven't learned how to work a video camera, and don't think they have the time to learn.

True, learning to use a camera will take a little time at first, but someone on your faculty probably has that knowledge and can teach you. Also, if the students sometimes get wound up when a camera is in the room, let them get used to it being there; they'll calm down, and really start doing some neat things. At any rate, once the initial obstacles are overcome, and once you are convinced that videos, filmstrips, slides, and photographs are viable learning tools, you will be amazed at how interesting an assignment can be for a group of students working on a media arts activity.

When dealing with media arts, don't forget the importance of the newspaper. Always accessible and inexpensive, using newspapers to stimulate a math lesson, language art assignment, science, or visual arts project, is another easy way to incorporate media arts into a daily lesson plan.

The following media arts activities are some of our favorites, ones that have been done successfully, time and time again, by students and teachers. So, find a director's chair, get a megaphone, blow the whistle, and yell, "Lights, Camera, Action!" Who knows. Maybe Steven Spielberg needs an assistant.

Homemade Filmstrips

GRADE LEVEL: 2-6

MATERIALS: overhead acetate transparencies cut into 2-inch strips
transparency markers or water based markers
transparent tape

AREA: classroom

TIME NEEDED: 1 hour

PURPOSE: To strengthen communication skills, to develop expression through use of the media arts, to practice working together, to review sequencing, to share research material with the class, to develop new vocabulary.

PROCEDURES:

1. After you have assigned your students a research project, use this activity as a means of presenting their findings. Assign the research project in groups of two or three. Explain that each group will be presenting their project information in the form of a filmstrip that includes drawings and dialogue.

2. Once the research is completed, direct the groups to create mock up strips of the pictures and dialogue they will have in their filmstrip *cells* (each section of the transparency that has a picture is a cell). That is, have them draw on a sheet of paper a strip with as many cells as they need in order to give their report and create the illustrations and dialogue. Cells can be made by drawing lines on the acetate strip, or folding the acetate strip into sections.

3. The acetate transparency sheet should be cut in two-inch strips and taped end to end to make it long enough for the report. Fold each strip to designate the cells.

4. Once the report ideas have been put on mock up strips, and all the changes have been made, allow the groups to create the real thing by using the transparency strips and markers. It is best for students to use markers that can be easily erased with a tissue in case of mistakes.

5. When filmstrips are complete, allow each group to present its strip on the overhead projector. Use a sheet of paper to cover all of the filmstrip cells except the cell that is being shown. For really fancy filmstrips, allow the students to tape record the dialogue with accompanying music. It adds polish to the presentation.

ACADEMIC VARIATIONS:

Math: Give students a strip and have them illustrate a math story problem. You may wish to ask one student to illustrate a problem, and have the rest of the class add the dialogue.

Creative Writing: Divide the class into pairs. One person draws a filmstrip, and the other person writes the dialogue based on the filmstrip.

Drug and Alcohol Abuse: Have the students illustrate the consequences of drug and alcohol abuse, how to say "no" to peer pressure, or the appropriate actions to take if a friend is involved with drugs.

FLOURISHES:

If your school has a program in which older students (5th or 6th grade) teach or tell stories to the first graders, filmstrips would make a great activity. Find out some of the first graders' favorite stories. Make your own filmstrips of those stories, using the same story lines, but changing the characters' names to those of students in the first grade class. Personalizing a story in this way is a real kick for the little ones. They'll never forget it.

Historical Headlines

GRADE LEVEL: 4-6

MATERIALS: newspaper sections
glue or tape
writing paper

AREA: classroom

TIME NEEDED: 45 minutes

PURPOSES: To find parts of speech in a newspaper story, to create an historical headline from a contemporary headline, to develop creative thinking, to promote creative writing skills, to construct an original story, to strengthen communication skills.

PROCEDURES:

1. Divide students into groups of two or three. Give each group a section of a newspaper, being sure to use only those sections with several headlines in them.

2. Take a section and read some headlines at random. Have the class discuss the actual meanings of the headlines. Then take an existing headline, for example, "Religion Issue Returns," and ask students to write a newspaper account of an historical event, using that headline. Remind students to use the five Ws (Who, What, Where, When, Why) in their articles.

3. When articles have been completed, allow students to share them with each other. They should be catalysts for good discussions on certain events in history. A sample of an historical article written for a current headline follows:

Religion Issue Returns

Wearing banners and carrying placards, a small group of Puritans once again paraded around the grounds of the palatial manor of King James I, and protested the extravagant way in which the Church of England is being run. Waving signs saying "Down with colorful robes," and "If God had wanted stained glass, He would have been an artist," the Puritans and their leaders asked King James for a charter to establish a colony somewhere in the New World.

King James, who has had to deal with this type of unrest for many months now, dismissed the group with a nod of the head and an exclamation of "good riddance," and told the protesters to settle in a place called the Massachusetts Bay Colony. Pooling their rather large resources, the well-to-do Puritans have begun readying ships for sail and will reach their new home sometime in 1620.

ACADEMIC VARIATIONS:

Reading: Using the same format, have students use a headline to rewrite a fairy tale or nursery rhyme.

Health or Science: Give students a headline. Ask half of the students to write a negative account of what that headline might mean. Ask the other half to write a positive account of the headline.

Environmental Education: Give students a headline. Ask them to think in terms of animals or inanimate objects (smoke, trash, factories, acid rain, and so on), and write an appropriate account in the first person. For example:

Cowboys Beat Eagles

I am an eagle and have lived in the forest all of my life in the top of a special tree. Yesterday, as I was swooping down close to the ground, I was captured in a net by a cowboy who wanted some of my feathers for his hat. This is a sad day, not just for me, but for all eagles everywhere.

FLOURISHES:

Give each group of students a section of the newspaper. Their job is to select three nouns, two adjectives, and one or two verbs at random, and write those words on a piece of paper. Give the pieces of paper to other groups, who must write a headline using all of the words. Then give the new headlines to new groups, who must write a newspaper account from the headline.

Lights, Camera, Action

GRADE LEVEL: 5-6

MATERIALS: cardboard boxes of different sizes
spotlight
film or slide projector
costumes
wigs
props

AREA: classroom or activity room

TIME NEEDED: 2 class periods

PURPOSE: To practice vocal projection, to practice staying in character, to express a written idea through drama, to create stage sets, to determine the value of good or bad journalism, to emphasize sequencing, to have fun.

PROCEDURES:

1. Lead a discussion on the different programming seen on television. Delve into the positive and negative aspects of televised sporting events, situation comedies, dramas, political panel shows, soap operas, news programs, television movies, talk shows, and commercials. Ask the students to select three or four programming formats and use them to describe historical events.

2. Have students decide which TV format they want to be a part of. Group students according to their choices and have them work sets, dialogue, action, and historical events appropriate to that format. The students who chose to work in the newscast segment will sit behind a desk, become anchorpersons, and deliver news that is pertinent to an event in history. The students who chose a soap opera will devise a skit that dramatizes an historical event. The talk show segment will offer a format which includes visiting celebrities who come onstage and discuss their roles in history with the host. The students who present commercials will advertise products that have to do with certain periods in history.

3. Divide the room into four areas, one for each segment. Sets will be constructed out of cardboard boxes, chairs, and posterboard. Each group will work independent of the others.

4. After the students have had rehearsal time, and the construction of the sets is complete, put up a filmstrip projector, slide projector, or spotlight in the back of the room. Have students take their places in their set and get ready to perform.

5. Darken the room and shine the spotlight on one scene at a time. Make sure the entire scene is lit, so that all of the students know which scene is on. The actors in that scene will present their show.

6. When all skits have been presented, a discussion on which situations worked and which didn't should follow. Focus on the TV program format the students feel was the most effective for getting information across.

ACADEMIC VARIATIONS:

Reading: Have students decide on four different children's stories. They will make sets to fit the particular stories and present those stories in the same manner as described above.

Health: Give the students a health topic, and have them present selected information to the audience using the different TV formats. As a variation, the teacher may want to give each group the same topic, and have each group use a different format to present the same information.

FLOURISHES:

Get the video camera, grab some costumes, and shake off the wigs. It's time for the six o'clock news. During the morning, ask your student reporters to go around the school and find breaking news stories. Let some students go outside and clock the wind, gauge the rain, and check for clouds, thunder, or snow. Sports reporters will go to the upper grades and get football scores, the outcomes of baseball games on the playground, or details on the competition in the gym.

Then your reporters will present their news on a news set complete with anchorpersons, weatherpersons, sportscasters, satellite reporters, and so on. Videotape the show, and give the tape to other classrooms for viewing.

Shoot a Mystery

GRADE LEVEL: 5-6

MATERIALS: 3 or 4 35mm cameras
print film
manila folders
transparent tape

AREA: classroom and playground

TIME NEEDED: several class periods

PURPOSE: To practice using a camera, to promote teamwork, to develop thinking skills, to demonstrate problem-solving techniques.

PROCEDURES:

1. Divide students into groups of three or four. Define each member's duties to prevent confusion. Individual duties include:

   photographer
   cataloguer (who will name characters and setting, and write a title for the project)
   biographer

2. Have students take the cameras and go around the school to other classrooms, the administrative offices, the janitor's closet, the cafeteria, and other places, and take pictures of six or eight people, and two or three shots of interesting places, such as inside a school bus, the teacher's workroom, or somewhere in the school cafeteria kitchen.

3. Once the film has been developed, all of the pictures should be taped to the inside of one or two manila folders, leaving space underneath each picture for a short biography of each character. The person in charge of naming the characters and sites give each person a fictitious name, and write the location names on the other side of the manila folder.

4. When writing the bios, the students should try to relate all of the characters in some way.

5. The next step is to title the mystery. Relate the title to the characters and sites.

6. Place all of this information in a manila envelope, and store alphabetically, according to title, in an easily accessible box.

7. Other students at their leisure can take out a packet, and write a mystery from the information provided. Remind students that once they begin to write the mystery, they must also solve it.

ACADEMIC VARIATIONS:

Reading: Have students use the same process as above, but use well-known characters from children's books when naming the characters and writing the bios. Some of the characters may come from one book, some from another. Write a story that includes all of these characters, using the information from the bios in writing or acting out the story.

Social Studies: Give each group a historical situation, and have them take pictures of characters that fit that particular historical event. Put all of the information into packets, and let other students try to rewrite history using the information in the folders.

FLOURISHES:

At the beginning of the year, have students put candid shots of themselves on the bulletin board. Have them write their own biographies. Underneath the biography, have students write a biography for themselves as they will be 20 years from now.

Slide/Tape/Story

GRADE LEVEL: 5-6

MATERIALS: 35mm camera
rolls of slide film
selection of musical cassette tapes
slide projector and carousel tray

AREA: classroom

TIME NEEDED: 2 or 3 class periods

PURPOSE: To tell stories through media arts, to promote teamwork, to practice creative writing skills, to solve problem situations.

PROCEDURES:

1. Divide the students into groups of four. Have each member choose a role for the project. The four main jobs are:

   photographer (shoots all film)
   narrator/scriptwriter (writes and narrates finished piece)
   music director (selects and tapes background music)
   scene director (finds and sets up scenes for story)

2. Direct each group to find a short story that they can use to create a slide presentation. They are to dramatize the story using slides that they take around the school or stage student actors. A class period may be required to select the story and assign responsibilities.

3. Once the story has been selected, give the students time to think of the way their group will illustrate the story. Groups may want to walk around the school looking for locations.

4. Ask each group to come up with a crude storyboard. This is a rough frame by frame sketch of what their story will be. These storyboards aid organization and keep kids on task.

5. Once the preliminary planning is completed, distribute the cameras and film. Ask parents to help you obtain enough cameras and film. Have groups photograph scenes to go along with their stories.

6. When the slides have been developed, have students put them in sequential order according to the particular story. Then have the assigned student write the script. Have the music director select appropriate background music, and the narrator practice reading the script.

7. The final job is to tape the music and narration to go with the slides. By now, the students should be so committed to their project that quality work will be the result.

ACADEMIC VARIATIONS:

Social Studies: Give groups of students different topics of discussion related to the community or the state in which they live, and have them make a slide show on that topic. This will require research and library time.

Health: The students could make a slide presentation relating to drug abuse or smoking, and present it to the student body or to a parent group.

FLOURISHES:

Give each group a roll of slide film, and have them take pictures of objects that begin with each of the letters of the alphabet.

Develop and categorize all of the slides. Put all of the *A* slides in one box, all of the *B* in another, and so on. Now students have a ready-made resource for creative writing, poetry, and other slide presentations.

Video Dialogue

GRADE LEVEL: 6

MATERIALS: video camera
writing paper
cassette player with microphone
blank tape

AREA: classroom

TIME NEEDED: 2 class periods

PURPOSE: To develop creative expression through video, to practice vocal projection and characterization, to promote teamwork, to develop critical thinking, to demonstrate problem-solving techniques.

PROCEDURES:

1. Have students rehearse a scene with a lot of action but no dialogue. This scene can take place in the classroom, on the playground, in the hallways, or anywhere in the school.

2. Videotape the scene in its entirety, without dialogue or noise.

3. Divide students into groups. Have them watch the silent video and write dialogue that fits the action. Remind them to concentrate on having a beginning, middle, and conclusion to their story.

4. Have the students rehearse the dialogue until it is comfortable to them. Then each group will speak the dialogue into the microphone as they watch the video. Timing is very critical here, so several attempts may be needed. As only one group can create the voice-over effects at a time, the teacher may want to schedule a time for each group in an unused room, so that there are fewer interruptions.

5. Have the groups play their video with accompanying dialogue. This can be a humorous way to see how dialogue and action really relate.

ACADEMIC VARIATIONS:

Reading: Have students write an original story, but leave it open-ended. Then have them act it out on video. Other students must write a conclusion to the story, and videotape the ending.

FLOURISHES:

Make a video *Alphabet Book* for a kindergarten or first grade class. Take the video camera, and going anywhere on school grounds, tape five things that begin with each letter of the alphabet. Have a narrator, or guide, say the name of the object several times. Lower grade classes can use the tape to review the letters of the alphabet.

Chapter 9

MUSIC

music (myü zik) *n.* 1: pleasing tones, sounds having rhythm, melody, or harmony 2: what Whitney Houston makes 3: without which life would be a mistake 4: response of the heart 5: a universal smile 6: energy 7: rhythm 8: fun.

Music is the one creative arts form that we seem to use in the classroom on a regular basis, at least during holidays. But then we leave the other 172 teaching days to the music teacher. Music is the true equalizer. It is a universal language. It can and should be an everyday occurrence in your classroom.

So how can we use music daily? What do we do with music when we teach math, or study Mexico, or learn about descriptive words? How can we include music when we panto-mime, or learn about the human body, or listen to a story?

First thing in the morning, before the students arrive, make a cassette of five or six good pieces of music, any and all kinds of music. Turn the cassette player on and leave it on all day. Turn it down when you are talking. Leave it comfortably low when the students are working. Let the music become an integral part of a well-rounded experience for your boys and girls.

Sing all the time. Give a short lesson in sing-song style. Rap. Beat on the desks. Let the students make up their own songs to describe personal situations. Teach them songs that you knew as a child. Bring in musical instruments. Let the students touch them, smell them, hold them. Show videos of orchestras, marching bands, jazz bands. Familiarize your class with well-known musicians, classic or contemporary. Learn songs from other countries, teaching appreciation of different musical styles. Allow the children to sing for the class, alone or in groups. Sing to them, sing with them. And never ever worry that you might not know where middle "C" is.

Years ago, someone gave us sweatshirts that said: *Without Music, Life Would Be a Mistake.* We couldn't have said it better.

Homemade Musical Instruments

Here's something fun to do with your kids—make homemade musical instruments. Let your class use these noisemakers to accompany stories, poems, or songs. If you have a selection of children's songs, or sing-a-long tapes, let the kids add their own accompaniment as they sing. Students tend to take ownership of an experience if they can be an integral part of that experience. The use of homemade instruments can do just that. Our favorites are:

Balloon Maraca	Blow up balloons of different sizes. Put five or six paper clips inside the blown-up balloon. Tie a knot in the balloon and shake. Kids may want to decorate the balloon after it is blown up. Beans, rice, and uncooked, rounded pasta also work well.
Pop Can Maraca	Drink a pop. Put a small amount of dried beans, beads, or rice in the empty can. Seal and cover the entire can with duct tape. Decorate. Shake.
	HINT: The correct way to hold a cylindrical type maraca is to hold hand palm up and place the can between your thumb and other fingers. Now visualize a big backward "C" in front of you with the open part of the "C" facing you. Make the shape of that backward "C" movement with your can beginning at the top of the "C" following down to the bottom of the "C." When you have done the movement slowly at first, then increase your speed until you have a steady rhythm and movement with your can.
Kazoos	Cut out a circle of wax paper about four inches in diameter. Place the circle of paper over the end of a toilet paper roll. Secure the paper as tightly as possible with a rubber band. Prick a tiny hole in the wax paper. Put your mouth over the open end of the cylinder and hum as you blow. Variation: Place a piece of wax paper over a comb. Hum and blow on the side of the comb that has no paper on it
Shoe Box Guitar	Get a shoe box, and discard the lid. Stretch several widths of rubberbands over the shoe box lengthwise, remembering to put the thicker rubber bands closer to you and to have them get thinner as they get farther away from you. Strum across the rubber bands. Sounds good.
Sandpaper Blocks	Go to a construction site, and gather short, discarded pieces of wood. Glue or staple pieces of sandpaper to one side of the wood. Slide two pieces of the wood against each other.

Coffee Can Bongos	Take two coffee cans of different sizes, and tape them securely side-by-side with duct tape. You can make different sounds by either thumping on the plastic lids, or the bottom of the can, or by taking the lid off and thumping on the bottom. Variation: Get four or five cans of different sizes and tape them together. Voila! An instant set of drums.
Paper Plate Tambourines	Put two paper plates together so that the concave sides of the plates are facing each other. Staple all around the edges, leaving a small space to drop in uncooked elbow macaroni. Staple the hole closed. Shake. Variation: Take one paper plate and cut out the center of the plate, leaving a two-inch edge all the way around. Using colored yarn, attach buttons, shells, bottle caps, or bells to the paper plate.

Percussion Instruments

Percussion instruments can be used with all age children. Because they are not toys, but well-constructed professional instruments used by musicians in orchestras, bands, and music groups, they will last a long time and are a good investment. Teach children how to handle the instruments gently. When not in use, they should be stored in a cloth-lined suitcase, duffel bag, or any container that will not allow them to get scratched or broken. Prices range from $6 to $35 or more per instrument. If one or two instruments are purchased each year, you will have a great collection in no time.

Percussion instruments have multiple uses. They work well for providing sound effects to enhance storytelling. And as accompaniment to singing, these instruments add flavor, whimsy, and fun to any song.

The following is a list of instruments that we have found to be a good addition to the classroom. Addresses of companies that carry percussion instruments can be found in the appendix under Catalogs (p. 210).

kazoo	triangle
tambourine	cymbals
flex-a-tone	wooden agogos
ratchet	slapstick
song whistle	siren whistle
metal tube shaker	cabasa
vibra slap	maracas
horse hoofs	train whistle
wind chimes	claves
bird whistle	wrist bells
finger cymbals	wood blocks
bongos	

Children's Musicals
How to Select; How to Write

To some teachers a children's musical means having tickets to see *Annie*. To others, it means watching grown people perform a musical play that is geared to the likes, tastes, and ages of young folk. To us, however, it means a story, with music, performed by children.

Sounds difficult, doesn't it? Sounds like something your kids would never buy into. Right? Wrong! It isn't all that hard to change an ordinary children's story like *Where the Wild Things Are* by Maurice Sendak into a musical that can be memorized and performed by your students. It's not only easy, it is something your class can help you do. How's that for a language arts lesson?

So, how do you write a script from a story? Here's how:

1. Find a well-known children's book, one your kids are familiar with—not too long, not too short, but just right.

2. Read through the story and count the number of main characters and minor characters. Remember, characters in children's books are not always animate. Characters may be talking sticks, trees, or furniture. The number of major and minor characters will be, loosely, the number of people that will make up your cast.

3. Go through the book again. Note the different places the story takes you. Are you in the forest? In a cave? On the ocean? Select three or four of the most important ones. These will be your scenes.

4. Read through the story again, this time a bit more thoroughly. Highlight all of the sentences that are not in quotes, give directions or descriptions, or set up a scene. Of these lines, those that are applicable and integral to the telling of the story will be the Narrator's lines.

5. Next, read through the story and highlight, in a different color, what each character says. All of these lines should have been written in quotes in the story. These are the characters lines in the script.

6. When writing the dialogue, put the action and emotion in parentheses. This is done to direct the actors in how to behave as they say their lines. Remember, words in parentheses are never read; they are acted out.

7. Once the character dialogue has been taken from the story, transitional lines can be added to beef up the characters or clarify what is taking place.

8. Script the entire story this way until you clearly know who says or does what, and when and how they say and do it.

9. Now add the music. First, you need to find the right spot in the play for a song or a dance. Songs and dances don't just go anywhere, they need a special place to have impact. Read the story once again and look for peaks or high points in the story that can be enhanced through song or dance. You decide where the music belongs.

10. If you have a flair for writing poetry, or if some of your students want to try, write a poem to turn into a song. The melody is the easiest part. You have two choices: use a well-known melody and fit the words to it, or you and your students (and maybe the music teacher for moral support) can work together and put the poem to an original tune. Yes you can!

11. If movement describes a peak better than a song will, let the characters dance. Kids love to make up dance steps, let them choreograph the dances. If original dance music is out of the question, as it usually is, decide what mood you're trying to impart, find a contemporary tape that fits that mood, and choreograph to that.

12. When presenting a children's musical, there is a place for everyone in your class to be involved. For some students, the stage may not be the place they want to be. That's why you have stage crews, house crews, and tech crews. Students on the stage crew close the curtain, change sets, cue actors during performances, and tear down, or strike, the sets when the performances are over. Tech crew students turn lights on or off, handle the spotlight (which might be nothing more than a slide projector with a blank slide that has had a round hole cut in it), and turn on the music at the appropriate times. The house crew is in charge of ushering and publicity.

13. You can be gutsy and creative and make your own musical play from a children's book, or you can purchase packaged plays for children. There are some good ones out there. We've listed some publishing companies for you in the appendix on page 211. Whichever route you take, our experience has shown that you must make all of the cast and crew selections before you present the idea to the students. You have final say on who, what, where, when, and why.

14. Now that all of the hard parts are behind you, it's time for rehearsal. Putting on a children's musical or play takes time if you do it right. So be prepared for that. Give your speaking parts out early. Most kids will have them memorized overnight. Block each scene, and show your actors how and where to move. Walking and talking at the same time sounds easy, but when it's done in a controlled, structured way it can take a little time to learn correctly.

15. Okay. The students are walking and talking at the same time. They've learned their lines, songs, and dances. They know when to turn the lights on, and when to play the music. It's a miracle, and you are a genius.

16. So, all that's left is the performance. Send out the invitations, set up the video camera, hush everybody backstage, and ... BREAK A LEG!

For your convenience, we have included an original musical for young children. It is a simple holiday theme, has many characters, and a few original songs that lend to the mood of the season.

Christmas Isn't Christmas Without a Tree

GRADE LEVEL:

LENGTH OF PLAY:

CAST LIST: (See cast form on p.162.)

Child 1	Tin Soldiers (6)	Tree 4
Child 2	Tin Soldier Leader	Tree 5
Child 3	Mrs. Claus	Susie Snowflake
Child 4	Lumberjack 1	Snowflake 1
Helper 1	Lumberjack 2	Snowflake 2
Helper 2	Lumberjack 3	Snowflake 3
Helper 3	Tree 1	Snowflake 4
Santa Claus	Tree 2	Snowflake 5
	Tree 3	Blocks (9)

PROP LIST AND SET DESIGNS:

SCENE 1: THE LIVING ROOM.

fireplace (painted backdrop or brick corrugated paper in shape of fireplace)

stocking hung on fireplace

unwrapped presents and packages on floor

3 chairs covered with afghan or bedspread to resemble couch

throw rug in front of couch

9 human alphabet blocks (cardboard box to fit partially over body or head, tempera paint to color boxes, black tempera paint to print letters on boxes)

SCENE 2: SANTA'S WORKSHOP.

2 tables

chair

telephone on table

workbench and hammer

assorted toys

assorted colored light bulbs

letter

SCENE 3: FOREST.

backdrop of trees (optional)

hatchet for Lumberjacks (optional)

SCENE 4: LIVING ROOM.

same as Scene 1

Christmas tree with lights

Costume List

Child 1   pajama, slippers.

Child 2   pajamas with feet, robe.

Child 3   pajamas, slippers.

Child 4   pajamas, slippers, robe.

Helper 1   pair red or green tights, red or green sweatshirt, red or green toboggan cap, one can WD-40, rope belt.

Helper 2   black tights, red sweatshirt, black toboggan cap, colored light bulbs, rope belt.

Helper 3   purple tights, pink or white sweatshirt, any color toboggan cap, small hammer, rope belt.

Nonspeaking Helpers   any color tights, sweatshirt, cap, rope belt.

Santa Claus   Santa suit.

Mrs. Claus   long dress, shawl, wire granny glasses, gray wig.

Tin Soldiers   black pants, white long-sleeve shirt, red suspenders, tall red hat with black brim made of construction paper, white gloves.

Tin Soldier Leader   same as Tin Soldier, white gloves, gold braids across shoulder.

Lumberjacks   rolled up jeans, plaid shirts, any color cap, suspenders, handkerchief.

Trees   green tights and turtlenecks, cardboard tree cutout with hole for face, green face makeup.

Snowflakes   white jeans or tights, white turtlenecks, white snowflake cutout mask made of posterboard and attached to head with elastic band.

Susie Snowflake   white tights, white skirt, white turtleneck, pink feather boa (optional).

Blocks   each block should have matching tights and sweatshirt, and the body box should be painted the same color. No two letters should use the same color, if possible. The letter should be written in black tempera or a black marker in bold strokes.

Cast List Form

Child 1 _____

Child 2 _____

Child 3 _____

Child 4 _____

Helper 1 _____

Helper 2 _____

Helper 3 _____

Santa Claus _____

Tin Soldiers (6) _____

_____

Tin Soldier Leader _____

Mrs. Claus _____

Lumberjack 1 _____

Lumberjack 2 _____

Lumberjack 3 _____

Tree 1 _____

Tree 2 _____

Tree 3 _____

Tree 4 _____

Tree 5 _____

Susie Snowflake _____

Snowflake 1 _____

Snowflake 2 _____

Snowflake 3 _____

Snowflake 4 _____

Snowflake 5 _____

Blocks (9) _____

_____

_____

_____

_____

Christmas Isn't Christmas
Without a Tree

SCENE 1: LIVING ROOM. *(Enter four children, quietly sneaking into the room, looking around.)*

Child 1:
Is it Christmas yet?

Child 2:
Oh, it must be. There is a stocking hanging there. *(Children run to stocking.)*

Child 3:
It's empty.

Child 1:
Then it's not Christmas.

Child 2:
Sure it is. Here are some packages. *(Children run to the packages.)*

Child 3:
But they're not wrapped.

Child 1:
Then it's not Christmas.

Child 2:
Sure it is. Just look at the Christmas tree. *(All look.)*

Child 3:
What Christmas tree?

Child 2:
There must be a Christmas tree. *(Children look frantically all over the room for the tree.)*

All:
Where's the Christmas tree?

Child 3:
It's not Christmas without a Christmas tree.

Child 2:
What shall we do? *(Begins to cry.)*
(Thinks momentarily.) Let's write Santa and tell him. He'll help. I know he'll help. Do you have some paper?

Children 2 and 3:
No!

Child 4:
Pencil?

Children 2 and 3:
> No!

Child 4:
> Then what are we going to do?
> *(All of the children look dejected.)*

All Children: *(Sing Dear Santa)*
> Dear Santa, where is the Christmas tree?
> Dear Santa, where did it go?
> Dear Santa, without a Christmas tree,
> Christmas isn't Christmas, you know.
>
> Dear Santa, where is the Christmas tree?
> Dear Santa, lovely and green.
> Dear Santa, without a Christmas tree,
> This whole day might just be Halloween.

Children 3 and 4:
> We have a stocking.

Children 1 and 2:
> No one wants a stocking.

Children 3 and 4:
> We have some presents.

Children 1 and 2:
> They don't have a bow.

All:
> Santa could help us,
> If we just could tell him.
> How to do it we don't know.
>
> *(Piano plays while children look sad. Child 1 looks at blocks on floor, has a grand idea, and begins arranging the blocks to spell D E A R   S A N T A.   Other children catch on and help with the arrangement.)*
>
> Dear Santa *(Blocks spin)*,
> Where is the Christmas tree?
> Dear Santa *(Blocks spin)*
> What do you say?

Children and Blocks:
> Dear Santa, without a Christmas tree,
> This is just like any other day.
> *(Piano song while children and blocks look off into distance, freeze. Blackout.)*
> *(All exit stage.)*

SCENE 2: SANTA'S WORKSHOP.

(Santa is working at his desk. Several of his helpers are working elsewhere onstage.)

Helper 1:

Well, Mr. C., the sled is in great shape. You know, it sure is amazing what a little squirt of WD 40 can do. That sled will take you anywhere now.

Santa Claus:

(Preoccupied, mumbles.) Good, er.... That's good.
(Helper 1 backs off and begins to work.)

Helper 2:

(Enters carrying colored light bulbs.) Mr. Claus, do you still want to go with red this year for Rudolph? I really think we should try something softer, maybe a yellow, or even pink. That would go nicely with his hair coloring and complexion.

Santa Claus:

(Mumbles, doesn't look up.) Mmmm, hm, ermmm....
(Helper 2 backs up and resumes work.)

Helper 3:

(Enters disheveled with smudges on face.) I quit.... I said I quit! I will not shoe those reindeer anymore. Mr. Claus, do you know that each one of those creatures has four feet? That's 48 shoes I have to put on. And with them laughing and giggling all the time.... Well, I can't do it. I simply can't do it.

Santa Claus:

(Still mumbling, not looking up from work at desk.) That's good. That's very good.
(Helper 3 backs up and resumes working.)
(Enter six tin soldiers and leader.)

Leader:

Hut, two, three, four, hut, two, three, four. Company ... halt! Well Boss, what do you think? Not bad, huh? And except for a leg falling off of one of them, I think they turned out very well. On time too. What do you think Boss?

Santa Claus:

(Mumbles but doesn't look up, tin soldiers and leader march off to another part of the stage.)
(Enter Mrs. Claus who walks over to Santa and bends down to him.)

Mrs. Claus:

Dear, is something wrong? I've never seen you like this so close to Christmas Eve. You seem a million miles away.

Santa Claus:

(Looks up.) Oh, Honey, I'm sorry. It's just this letter. I got it today and it has me worried. *(Hands letter to Mrs. Claus.)*

Mrs. Claus:

(Reads letter silently.) No Christmas tree. Well that is a problem, the poor little dears. What on earth shall we do? *(Both think for a few seconds.)*

Mrs. Claus:

How about Wal-Mart? I hear they make little trees out of tin now. In all colors. Maybe a nice orange....
(Santa Claus stares at her and shakes his head in disbelief at such an idea.)

Mrs. Claus:

(Still thinking.) Can you still get things with green stamps? I've had a book of those things saved for years. Thought about getting a lamp at one....
(Santa Claus cuts off her sentence with a deadly stare.)

Mrs. Claus:

Macramé?
(Santa shakes head no.)

Mrs. Claus:

Kleenex and chicken wire?

Santa Claus:

(Stands. Shakes head.) No, it's got to be a real tree. An honest-to-goodness tree. And I hear they're not growing too well this year because it's been so dry. We've got a disaster on our hands, a real disaster.
(Begins to pace back and forth, back and forth.) Think! I want everybody to think!!
(Everyone onstage assume a thinking pose.)
(All sing: "Where Will We Find a Christmas Tree for Christmas?," pp. 172-174.)

Santa Claus:

I've got it!

Helpers and Mrs. Claus:

(Look at audience.) He's got it!

Santa Claus:

Get me Susie Snowflake. QUICK! *(Picks up phone from desk.)*
(Blackout. All exit stage.)

SCENE 3: FIELD OF DROOPY, SAD-LOOKING CHRISTMAS TREES.
(Three lumberjacks walk through the forest checking out trees.)

Lumberjack 1:

Do you see any trees we need to cut?

Lumberjack 2:

Nah. These are all too small and droopy. We'll just let the sun dry them out some more and chop them up for kindling.

Lumberjack 3:

I'm for just letting them rot, they're so pitiful looking.
(Lumberjacks nod heads and exit.)
(Trees look at each other.)

Tree 1:

(Hands on hips.) Pitiful? Did you hear him? He said pitiful. Is that what we are? Pitiful? *(Looks at himself.)*

Tree 2:

I'm afraid so. If we don't get some moisture soon, we might as well be kindling. Maybe the man was right. *(Begins crying.)*

Tree 3:

(Begins sobbing too.) Boo hoo hoo. Boo hoo hoo.

Tree 4:

No, no, no.... Don't cry. Something has to change. We're not out of the woods, yet, but something will change. I know it. I just know it.

Tree 5:

Let's try stretching our toes deeper into the ground to see if we can touch some water. *(Trees wiggle and struggle, then all start softly weeping.)*
(Trees sing "Christmas Is Coming," *pp. 175-178.)*

(Piano ends the melody slowly. As song ends, trees sniff and try to hug each other.)
(Offstage noise of trampling and walking.)
(Snowflakes begin dialogue offstage.)

Snowflake 1:

Are you sure you know where you're going, Susie? We've been walking for hours.

Susie Snowflake:

Santa said go about a mile, turn left at the old cabin, keep going North past the frozen pond, then on past the bear's cave, and we can't miss them.

Snowflake 2:

But that was three miles ago.

Snowflake 3:

They've got to be around here somewhere.

Snowflake 4:

Hey, what's that up ahead? Could be those trees we're looking for.

Snowflake 5:

Who can tell? They all look alike to me. If you've seen one tree, you've seen them all.
(Susie enters, other snowflakes follow.)

Susie Snowflake:

(Susie walks around trees.) Well, we finally found you. And, boy, are you a sight for sore eyes.
(Other snowflakes nod agreement.)

Tree 1:

A sight for sore eyes. Now wait a minute. What's going on here?

Susie Snowflake:

Santa sent us down here to help you guys out. You know, moisture and all. *(All snowflakes rub their bodies.)*

Tree 2:

It'll never work. We're finished.

Tree 3:

We're headed for that great kindling bundle in the sky. I know it. It's twig heaven for us. *(All trees ad lib "Yea," "That's Right," "That's it," "Uh huh.")*

Susie Snowflake:

Enough of that kind of talk. We're here to help you. Right troops?

All Snowflakes:

Right.

Susie Snowflake:

Ten hut! *(Snowflakes march forward.)* Halt! *(Snowflakes stop and gather around each tree.)* Now, ... MELT!

(As snowflakes dissolve around trees, trees begin standing straighter and taller. Trees look around at each other.)

Tree 4:

You did it! You made us grow again. Now we can be Christmas trees. Real honest-to-goodness Christmas trees.

Susie Snowflake:

(Standing up.) Nothing to it. Just a squeeze here. A drip there. All in a day's work.

Tree 5:

How do we thank you? How can we ever repay you?

Susie Snowflake:

By getting out of here and doing your thing. Christmas, remember? Tinsel, stars, presents, children, all that stuff. You know, Christmas?

All Trees:

Christmas, oh yes, yes, yes! *(All trees jump up and down.)*
(Snowflakes rap "Hurry, Hurry, Hurry," p. 179.)

(Trees exit running. Blackout.)

SCENE 4: LIVING ROOM. *(4 children enter in darkness.)*

Child 3:

Is it Christmas?

Child 2:

I don't see any lights.

Child 1:

Well then, it's not Christmas.

Child 4:

Let's go in the living room anyway.

Child 2:

Why? It's not Christmas.

Child 4:

You're right. It's not Christmas.

Child 1:

I'm going to peek just to make sure.
(Christmas tree lights go on, and full stage lights on. Children run into room and see tree, clap hands, rush to tree.)

Child 2:

It's really, really Christmas, isn't it?

Child 4:

Yes. *(Smiling.)* It's really really Christmas.
(All cast members come onstage and sing finale, "It's Amazing," pp. 180-181.)

The End
(Blackout.)
(Up lights. All cast members bow.)

Dear Santa

Words & Music by
Martha Brady

Copyright 1992 Martha Brady

Where Will We Find a Christmas Tree for Christmas?

Words & Music by
Martha Brady

Copyright 1992 Martha Brady

Christmas Is Coming

Words & Music by
Martha Brady

Piano Solo

Hurry, Hurry, Hurry

A Rap

by Martha Brady

You must hurry, hurry, hurry

You've got special things to do

We can't sit like this forever, don't you see (snap, snap)

Shake your branches, get the lead out

Time's a wasting, don't you know

You're not kindling now

You're each a Christmas tree (snap, snap)

Bend your arms and shake your body

Feel your top and make a point

Dance around and say it's great to be alive (clap, clap)

Better scram, please don't be tardy

Time for you to leave this joint

There are kids out there who want to see you shine (snap, snap)

You must hurry, hurry, hurry

You must hurry, hurry, hurry

Better hurry, hurry, scram

Get out of here.

It's Amazing

Words & Music by
Martha Brady

Copyright 1992 Martha Brady

Chapter 10

UNITS, TOPICS & THEMES

units (yü nits) *n.* 1: parts that perform a particular function.

topics (tä piks) *n.* 1: subjects treated in a speech or conversation.

themes (thēms) *n.* 1: subjects of artistic works.

units, topics, themes *n.* 1: putting it all together 2: skipping across the content area 3: using all the senses 4: discovering all sides 5: the nitty-gritty 6: thoroughness 7: energy 8: fun.

Units, topics, and themes are integrated methods of teaching a certain subject in a variety of complementary ways. Our students learn about bears by reading about bears, making bears, becoming bears, counting bears, visiting bears, singing about bears, writing about bears, and everything else, short of actually moving in with one of the animals. In learning about our state, we color the state flower, sing the state song, memorize the state motto, draw the state map, list the state cities, read about the state crops, write about the state heroes and build dioramas of our state's night sky. And the method works. The kids love it. They remember. They ask for more. They get excited. They are challenged. They explore, and they begin to see things around them in a thematic sense.

Unit or thematic study can be done in packets, centers, blocks, small groups, large groups, short periods of time, longer periods of time, with another teacher, daily, weekly, or yearly.

The best way to decide on what topic or theme to pursue is to listen to your students. What are their interests? What kinds of books do they read? Has something unusual happened to them over the summer, during the weekend, at Grandma's house? What strange questions do they ask? What are they fascinated by or keep coming back to in discussions? Pay attention to all of these clues, then draw conclusions, make some decisions, and begin planning the curriculum with your class. Working together empowers your students and offers them choices.

The following units of study are geared for the inclusion of a variety of creative arts disciplines. They include areas of creative writing, music, dance and movement, drama, storytelling, and visual arts.

Color

GRADE LEVEL: 2-6

MATERIALS: paper plates
     art paper
     Pyrex bowl
     assorted food colors
     vegetable oil
     costumes and props
     tempera paint
     cut up pieces of sponges (optional)

AREA: classroom

TIME NEEDED: 1 week

PURPOSE: To use different creative arts methods to describe, recognize, acknowledge, and appreciate color in our daily lives.

PROCEDURES:

Before presenting these creative arts activities dealing with color, children should have already been introduced to information regarding *basic colors*, *primary colors*, *secondary colors*, *complementary colors*, and *hues*. Words such as *color value*, *color intensity*, *tint*, and *shade* should have also been included in the general lessons on color.

The following are activities which will enhance your class's appreciation and understanding of the importance of color in our daily lives. Begin each new unit of study with some good children's literature. These are just a few of the wonderful books on color that can be used to introduce this topic to your boys and girls: *Mouse Paint* by Ellen Stoll Walsh, *Seven Blind Mice* by Ed Young, *Color* by Christina Rossetti, *A Color of His Own* by Leo Lionni, *Color Dance* by Ann Jonas, *Planting a Rainbow* by Lois Ehlert, and *Purple, Green and Yellow* by Robert Munsch.

Warm-up to Color Unit

1. Have students look at the clothing they are wearing and decide which color is most dominant. Group them with other students who have selected the same color. Lead a class discussion on prisms and rainbows, and review the order of color found in prisms or rainbows. Remember, a good way for students to recall the order of the colors is the acronym, ROY G. BIV (red, orange, yellow, green, blue, indigo, violet).

2. Have students line up in rows according to the colors of the rainbow, using the dominant color they are wearing to decide where to stand.

Movement and Color

1. Using tempera, paint a swatch of color on several paper plates. Include white and black in this activity. Show one colored plate at a time, and ask students to look at the color, think of an object that is that color, and move around the room as that object would move.

2. Show another colored plate again, but, this time ask the students to think of a mood that this color makes them think of. Ask the students to show that emotion through movement.

3. Now divide the students into groups of three or four. Show the class a colored plate, and ask each group to move in a way the color makes them feel, or as an object of the same color. Black and white plates can be included also.

Colored Coded Sentences

1. Give each member of a group of five or six students a colored plate. The students will, one at a time, be responsible for telling one section of the story, using their particular colored plate as a catalyst for their part of the story. For example:

   Student 1 (black)   "It was a very dark night."

   Student 2 (red)   "I was very angry because I couldn't find my tennis shoes."

   Student 3 (green)   "I walked to the woods thinking I might have left them there."

   Student 4 (blue)   "I came back to the house and asked my mom if she had seen them. She said she had washed them."

   Student 5 (white)   "I ran down to the basement, looked into the washing machine, and there they were, nice and clean."

2. As students tell their stories, have them hide their color from the audience, who must guess which color is being used.

Visual Arts and Color

1. On an overhead projector, place a glass bowl that has been filled with one cup water and one-half cup vegetable oil. Slowly put drops of food coloring into the mixture so the children can see what happens to colors when they mix, blend, or stand alone.

2. With this stimulus, the students can imitate what they see by using art paper and tempera paints or cut-up pieces of sponge and watercolors.

Creative Writing and Color

1. Ask students to get in groups of five or six, look at their own paintings, and on the back of the picture, write down the title of their picture.

2. Then have students take turns writing, one sentence at a time, a collective story about each of the pictures. Remember to stress logic and correct sequencing.

3. When the students have completed all of the stories, ask for volunteers to read some of them. The class should look at the pictures and discuss how the stories tie into the pictures themselves.

Drama and Color

1. Have students work in groups of four or five, and create short, informal skits about colors. By using the "Begin It" and "End It" format, each group will decide what sentence to use to begin or end the skit. Following are suggested sentences:

End It sentences:

"So that's why the sun is yellow."

"Well, I am sure about one thing, I will never buy a red shirt again."

"Thank you Mr. President, I will treasure this purple robe as long as I live."

"It's a good thing someone painted it silver."

"Well, I can see now why the black door has been locked."

Begin It sentences:

"Hey Mom, there's someone at the door in a pink bunny costume."

"Pardon me, but I can't help but notice that you have green hair."

"Yes, ground control, it does look like a blue marble with a giant purple dot."

"Attention, will the owner of a gold Volkswagen please go to the gorilla cage?"

"Well, teacher, when I opened up my lunch, there it was, red stuff all over my sandwich."

2. Be sure to provide scarves, wigs, masks, costumes, and other props to enhance this creative adventure.

Music and Color

Conclude this topic with some good old-fashion singing. The music teacher in your building should have many songs about color to choose from. If not, let the kids make up their own. Just write down on the chalkboard several song titles with familiar tunes. (For example: "Twinkle, Twinkle, Little Star," "Three Blind Mice," "Oh, Susannah," "Row, Row, Row Your Boat," "This Land Is Your Land.") Now let the kids write any kind of song they want as long as it has to do with some color. Students can work individually or in pairs.

Here is a sample of original songs using well-known melodies:

My House Is Purple ("This Land Is Your Land")

My house is purple, my car is blue

My dog is yellow, my cat is too.

In the land of make-believe, all this is true.

Oh, won't you come and look with me.

The sky is orange, the clouds are brown.

The grass is fuchsia, flat on the ground.

In the land of make-believe, all this is true.

Oh, won't you come and look with me.

Purple Pink in My Sink ("Edelweiss")

Purple pink in my sink. I just spilled my tempera

Green and blue on my shoe, I'm so bummed they were brand new.

Orange and red spilled on my head. Now I look like a carrot.

Black and brown all around, I don't think I can bear it.

Clouds of the Storm ("The Wheels on the Bus")

The clouds of the storm are blue and purple, blue and purple, blue and purple,

The clouds of the storm are blue and purple, all around the world.

The green grass grows when the rain comes down, rains come down, rains come down.

The green grass grows when the rain comes down, all around the world.

The colors of the rainbow, red, orange yellow, red, orange yellow, red, orange, yellow.

The colors of the rainbow, red, orange, yellow, all around the world.

When the rain doesn't come there is no color, is no color, is no color.

When the rain doesn't come there is no color, all around the world.

The Messy, Messy Painter ("Itsy Bitsy Spider")

The messy, messy painter came out to paint my house.

He didn't pay attention. Oh, such a foolish louse.

First he spilled the yellow, and then he spilled the red.

When I saw my orange house, I nearly lost my head.

Grandmothers and Grandfathers

GRADE LEVEL: 3-6

MATERIALS: posterboard
markers or crayons
hand props such as scarves, balloons, rubber balls, pieces of cloth, masks, paper
plates
stool
selection of wigs, costumes
cardboard boxes or chairs

AREA: classroom or activity room

TIME NEEDED: 2 weeks

PURPOSE: To use different creative arts methods to describe, recognize, and acknowledge important family members such as grandmothers and grandfathers.

PROCEDURES:

Oral History and Storytelling

1. Begin this unit by reading aloud to the students one or two children's books that have to do with grandparents. Some of our favorites are *Grandma's Joy* by Eloise Greenfield, *A Grandmother's Story* by Glenn Halak, *Annie and the Old One* by Miska Miles, *Grandpa's Song* by Tony Johnston, *The Family of Grandparents* by Maria Rius and J. M. Parramon (in Spanish and English), *Song and Dance Man* by Karen Ackerman, *My Grandma's Chair* by Maggie Smith, *A Visit to Grandma's* by Nancy Carlson, and *Georgia Music* by Helen V. Griffith.

2. Ask four volunteers to come to the front of the room one at a time, sit on a stool, and describe their grandparent's house. Ask them to speak slowly, enunciate, and use as many descriptive words as they can to accurately describe the house to the other students in the class. Read the following passage to illustrate to your class just how much detail they need to include in their descriptions of their own grandparent's house.

3. The other students in the class cannot ask questions at this point. They must only listen and remember what is being said.

My Grandmother's House
by Martha Brady

My grandmother lived out in the country. Her house was off of a red dirt road and up on a little hill. The house was made of wood, painted white, and had a tin roof. It had a wide, open hall that when right through the middle of the house. Two bedrooms were on the left of the hall, and the living room, kitchen, bathroom and another bedroom were on the right side. There was a long front porch that stretched entirely across the front of the house. At one end of the porch was a swing hung from long, silver chains that rattled when the swing moved. On the porch were three heavy, wooden rocking chairs, each with a brightly stuffed pillow covering the hard wooden slats that made up the seat. In front of one of the oversized chairs was a small short footstool.

The late afternoon would always find my grandfather in one rocking chair, my tiny grandmother in the rocker with the small footstool, and a big bowl of unshelled black eyed peas resting on the seat of the third rocker, each pod waiting to be popped open by my grandmother's frail, darkly-veined hands.

The yard in front of the house was covered with yellow daffodil flowers and sweet-smelling grass. There was one big bush at the edge of the house that had little green and white berries on it. The bush had a wonderful clean fragrance that made the air around it seem fresh, and when you rubbed your hands on the thick, prickly clumps that made up the bush, the smell would stay with you for days. When my cousins and I would play hide and seek, I would crawl up into the bush and sit very still, so that I was never found. I was always safe there.

Visual Arts

1. Before the four volunteers begin describing their grandparents' houses, divide the class into groups of four or five students. Assign each group to one of the storytellers. Ask the groups to sit together on the floor around one piece of white poster board, and each group should have different colored markers. Each poster board should have a line drawn across it about two-thirds down.

2. As the storytellers sit on the stool in front of the class, and give their descriptions, the group assigned to that speaker will draw the house being described. The group members cannot ask each other or the storyteller questions as they draw. Rather, they must work collectively to draw what their storyteller is describing. Remind students to leave the area below the line blank.

3. Once all four storytellers have presented their descriptions, and all four groups have completed their drawings, collect and redistribute them so that each group gets a drawing other than their own.

Creative Writing

1. With the new picture of a house in front of them, groups will discuss among themselves what events might have occurred in that house. Give the groups time to think of one event to write about. Remind them to look at every part of the picture, allowing what they see to give them ideas about what could have happened there.

2. Each group writes a story, in the blank space, about an event that happened in the house. The story must make sense, have a beginning, middle, and an end, and fit in the space provided.

3. Once all four groups have completed their drawings, they are redistributed so that each group gets a new drawing and story.

Drama

1. Now each group has a new picture and story to enjoy. Direct them to read the new story, look at the drawing of the house that goes with the story, and then create a way that they can act out the story with costumes, wigs, scarves, and tables and chairs for props.

2. Give the groups time to plan and rehearse. They may choose to act out the scene verbally or nonverbally. One person in each group can narrate the story as the others act it out, or students in the groups can take turns reading all of the parts in the story. Verbal interpretations require the students to stretch a bit more, but nonverbal retellings are certainly appropriate. You may want to set up the video camera for this activity.

3. Once all four groups have completed their skits, posterboards will be collected one last time and redistributed so that each group gets a new drawing.

Movement

1. This next to last installment of the Grandparent unit may be the most difficult thus far, but one you certainly want to include so that the children can have another sensory method to describe their grandparents.

2. Now you want students to begin to connect all that they have learned, from the initial story, to the drawing of the house, to the telling of an event, to the acting out of that event. Some picture, some moment, some memory, some feeling should emerge. Talk about those memories or feelings. Share a moment form your own childhood that has to do with your own grandparent's house. Allow students time to touch, taste, smell, see, hear.

3. Select one of the stories that the children wrote, or a story about your own grandparent's house, or read a book about grandparents. Give each student a hand prop to use such as a scarf, balloon, feather, elastic strip, rubber ball, or crepe paper streamer. Explain that as you read the story, they will act out what they hear through movement. They will use the prop in their hand to help tell the story of their movement as they do it.

4. Be clear with your expectations and rules. Make sure the space provided for this part of the unit is big enough for this activity. Dim the lights, make certain the children have enough individual space, play some appropriate music, and begin reading the selected story. The children will move accordingly.

Music

1. End this wonderfully eclectic unit with a song about Grandmother's House. The students may want to write their own words to existing tunes, or learn a new song from your selection of children's songs, or perhaps sing the one provided for you beginning on the following page. Once you have finished singing the song, invite real grandparents to come in and spend the morning with their grandchildren and share stories about what really happened in Grandmother's or Grandfather's house.

Grandmother's House

Words & Music by
Martha Brady

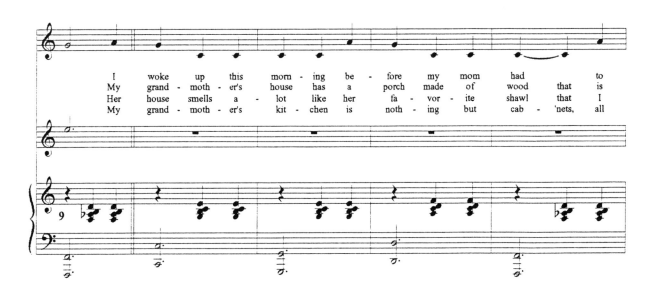

I woke up this morn - ing be - fore my mom had to
My grand - moth - er's house has a porch made of wood that is
Her house smells a - lot like her fa - vor - ite shawl that I
My grand - moth - er's kit - chen is noth - ing but cab - 'nets, all

*Note - The melody and the optional instrumental lines could be played by
flutes or oboes. Players should feel free to embellish, ornament, and/or ad lib
these parts. Percussion could also be added.

Copyright 1992 Martha Brady

Copyright 1992 Martha Brady

Copyright 1992 Martha Brady

Copyright 1992 Martha Brady

The Ocean

GRADE LEVEL: 3-6

MATERIALS: listed at the beginning of each segment

AREA: classroom

TIME NEEDED: 3 days to 2 weeks

PURPOSE: To demonstrate knowledge of the ocean and its environment through arts activities, to read, write, speak, and listen about the ocean, to express creatively, to work together, to demonstrate completion of projects.

Warm-ups and the Ocean

MATERIALS: rolls of colored cellophane
1-inch wide balsa wood strips
duct tape
cellophane tape

PROCEDURES:

1. Connect two long pieces of blue and green colored cellophane together with transparent tape. Place the green strip on top and the blue strip on bottom. Attach the joined pieces onto a simple wooden frame with duct tape. Be sure the cellophane paper is stretched as tight as possible on the wooden frame without tearing.

2. Prop the framed piece between two chairs or ask two students to hold it up. Stand behind the cellophane piece and tell the students that it is a large aquarium. Reviewing what happens to motion at certain depths because of the pressure of the water, become a fish, and move as it would under water. Become a crab, a shark, a cave.

3. Now ask students to come up, one at a time, or in small groups, and become something, animate or inanimate, that can be found under the water. The students might choose to be a lobster, an eel, an old tire, or a treasure chest. Several children might join together and become an octopus, a squid, or a jellyfish.

4. Direct some of the sea creatures to enter and exit the aquarium while others remain rigidly in the aquarium. Show them how to interact with each other, how a school of fish would swim among the kelp fronds, how an octopus would hide in a cave, and how a family of sea otters would dine on oysters and abalone.

Movement and the Ocean

MATERIALS: list of creatures or objects found in or near the ocean
long pieces of cloth that are blue or green in color
cassette tape of ocean sounds

PROCEDURES:

1. Find an open space. On the chalkboard, write a list of creatures or objects that can be found on the ocean floor, in the ocean, or near the shore.

2. Ask two pairs of students to take the long pieces of cloth and, holding them by the ends, wave the cloth up and down. Have the two pairs stand side-by-side and wave the cloths to duplicate the motion of waves. The visual effect is even stronger if there are four pieces of cloth moving at the same time but at different intervals.

3. As the ocean movement continues, ask six or seven students at a time to look on the board, select a creature or object, and move through the ocean as that creature or object would. After about 20 seconds, ask those students to find a position among the waves and remain there. Ask six or seven more students to do the same thing, until all of the students have had a chance to play among the waves and find their place in the ocean.

4. An added ingredient is the ocean sound effects tape. Play it at the beginning, and let it continue throughout this movement activity.

HINT: Plastic tablecloth rolls in a wide selection of colors can be purchased inexpensively at specialty stores that carry party supplies and picnic items. Environmental tapes can be purchased at most large discount record stores, and colored cellophane rolls can be found at most business supply stores, or art supply stores.

Visual Arts and the Ocean

MATERIALS: wax paper
construction paper
scissors
glue
string
butcher paper
newspapers
coffee filters
water based markers
plastic margarine containers

PROCEDURES:

Window Aquarium

1. Give students two pieces of wax paper of the same size. Direct them to cut from construction paper, three or four shapes of objects or creatures that can be found in the ocean.

2. Have students place the shapes on one piece of the wax paper, fastening them with glue.

From *Artstarts.* Copyright © 1994. Teacher Ideas Press, P.O. Box 6633, Englewood, CO 80155-6633.

3. Then place the second sheet over the shapes and tape the two pieces together at the edges.

4. Have the students tape the wax paper to a window, so that light can diffuse through the wax paper, and give it the effect of an aquarium.

Submarine Portholes

1. Give students a coffee filter or a piece of paper towel that has been cut in a circle.

2. Ask them to color the filter in any design, using water based markers. Tell them that the more color they put on the filters, the more vivid the final result.

3. Fill margarine containers with a small amount of water, and ask the students to dip the edges of the coffee filters into the water, rotating the filter around and around until the water begins to bleed the colors together.

4. Put the filters on a piece of newspaper until they are thoroughly dry, and then tape them on the windows, or hang them on a bulletin board.

Stuffed Sea Creatures

1. Using the same list that was generated for the "Movement and the Ocean" activity, ask students to select one sea creature or object found in the sea.

2. Have the students draw an outline of their sea creature or object on a folded piece of butcher paper or construction paper, depending on the size of the object. Have the children cut out their drawing, resulting in two identical shapes, because of the folded paper.

3. Now students decorate both sides of their cutouts, and then staple, tape, or glue the edges of the pieces together, leaving a small opening to stuff crumpled up newspaper inside. Seal the opening after the cutout has been stuffed.

4. Ask the students to use a hole punch to make a hole in the top of the stuffed creature. Attach a string so that it can be hung.

Creative Writing and the Ocean

1. Select a relatively empty corner of the room, and suspend looped sections of green and blue crepe paper from the ceiling, hanging the loops in different lengths so as to give the effect of waves in an ocean. On the walls behind the crepe paper, hang blue or green butcher paper as a background. Place a table underneath the hanging crepe paper strips. For effect, tape a piece of brown or tan butcher paper to the top of the table and sprinkle cornmeal on top of it. This makes good sand.

2. Help your students attach their creatures to the ceiling with pushpins, straight pins, or tacks, allowing the creatures to hang freely among the waves. Have the students place items that don't float or swim on the table.

3. Give your class time to look at their piece of the ocean, then have them write a story about one of the creatures or objects and how it got there, or how it relates to the other ocean inhabitants.

Drama and the Ocean

1. Go to a paint store and buy a clear plastic drop cloth. Find yet another space in your room that is somewhat uncluttered. Spread the drop cloth out and hang it from the ceiling using pushpins, staples, or string. Pull it down so that it is taut. Lay a long piece of board on the bottom edge of the cloth to hold it in place. You now have another instant aquarium.

2. Keep the space behind the hanging drop cloth free of any objects, as that will be the performing space.

3. Divide students into groups, and have them write their own ocean scene, and perform it as though they were under water. This environment is also a great place to read an ocean theme children's book or poem.

4. If the children are having trouble thinking of ideas to use as informal drama scenes, although that is unlikely, here are a few possible titles to get them going:

    "The Day the Octopus Broke His Arm"
    "What's in the Cave?"
    "Sharks!"
    "The Lost Pearl"
    "Lost in the Kelp Forest"
    "The Fish Who Swam Backwards"
    "Look! A Treasure Chest"
    "The Jellyfish Slumber Party"
    "The Wreckage of the Old Ship"
    "The Tiny Mermaid"

Sound

GRADE LEVEL: K-6

MATERIALS: pretaped selection of various kinds of music and sound effects
art paper
tempera paint or crayons

AREA: classroom

TIME NEEDED: 2 weeks

PURPOSE: To use different creative arts methods to describe, recognize, and appreciate color in our daily lives.

PROCEDURES:

As with the unit on color, students should be introduced to the whole concept of sound. What is sound? How is it produced? What are molecules? What does the word *vibration* mean? What are the parts of an ear? How do deaf people hear? What are *pitch*, *tone*, and *timbre*?

Experiments such as speaking through one end of a straw while listening through the other end, pulling a string very tight and watching it vibrate, or putting your finger in water to see the ripples will reinforce the concept of sound before the creative arts activities are introduced. Good children's books that you can use to introduce this unit include, *The Listening Walk* by Paul Showers, *Sound Words* by Joan Hanson, and *More Sound Words* also by Joan Hanson.

WARM-UPS:

1. Ask students to find a comfortable place in the room, close their eyes, and listen. After a minute or so, have them name the sounds they heard during that time, and explain where they think the sounds came from. Now ask them to close their eyes and listen once more. This time add some sounds, like blowing up a balloon, turning on a radio, and bouncing a ball. Have the students name the sounds they heard, and then discuss which sounds didn't fit into the classroom environment.

2. Have groups of students act out a scene using sounds to identify the location. One example would be the seashore. While most of the students lie on the floor with their eyes closed, the group of actors would make noises that are appropriate to the seashore, like waves crashing, seagulls calling, a foghorn bellowing, a crab scratching the sand, seals flapping, and so on. The sounds should continue for a fairly long time so that the rest of the students can internalize what they are hearing before opening their eyes. Other suggested situations are: a carnival midway, cooking breakfast, center ring at a circus, a jungle, a haunted house at Halloween, feeding time at the zoo, traffic in a large city, the Superbowl.

HINT: To make this activity a bit more difficult, you may want to ask the students to refrain from using words while making their sounds.

VISUAL ARTS AND SOUND:

1. Make a tape of short segments of different types of music, some soft and mellow, some with heavy bass and percussion lines, and some with flute and woodwinds. Interspersed between the segments tape random sounds such as a scream, a loud bass drum thud, or an airplane taking off.

2. Students will need art paper and crayons or tempera paint. As they listen to the tape they are to draw what they hear by using straight lines, curves, bold swaths, circles, streaks, ziggles, and other abstract forms to describe the sounds.

3. Using the sound words under "Movement and Sound" ask the students to take each word, and draw a symbol that represents that word. For example, a student might draw squiggly lines for the word *sizzle*, a pair of teeth for the word *chomp*, insect wings for the word *buzz*, a broken twig for the word *snap*, a pair of boots for the word *stomp*, a rocket for the word *blast*, or a snake for the word *hiss*.

CREATIVE WRITING AND SOUND:

1. Take the students outside, and ask them to sit still and listen to the sounds around them. Give them a few seconds to acclimate to the environment, and then to begin concentrating on what they hear. Have them write down the first 10 sounds they hear. Now have them write a story, poem, rap, or cinquain incorporating those 10 sounds.

2. Play a tape of various sound effects. Ask the students to listen to each segment and write down a memory that comes to mind when particular sounds are heard.

3. Take the class outside again. With a list of the letters of the alphabet in front of them, ask the students to listen for sounds that begin with different letters of the alphabet. Have them make a list of those sounds. Now go back to the room and compare sounds.

MOVEMENT AND SOUND:

1. Ask students to make a list of words that imitate sounds (*onomatopoeia*), words such as:

    crash sizzle crunch
    blast clomp chomp
    roar bang burst
    zoom splat creep
    creak boom buzz
    snap fizz hiss
    jangle punch stomp

2. Have students make a sound card for each word, then let them take turns holding up their cards and asking other students to move like those particular sounds.

DRAMA AND SOUND:

1. Divide students into groups of four or five. Play one sound for each group, and ask them to create a skit around that sound.

2. Play sounds that are unfamiliar to the students, or not easy to identify, such as the sound of a washing machine, of a jackhammer, a mosquito, or a landing helicopter. As you play the sounds, have the children pantomime what they think they are hearing.

The Anasazi

GRADE LEVEL: 4-6

MATERIALS: construction paper
markers
shadow puppet screen
long pieces of brown or tan butcher paper
tempera paints of red, yellow, blue, brown, black
Native American flute music
flashlights with red cellophane wrap covering the top to diffuse the light

AREA: classroom or activity room

TIME NEEDED: 2 or 3 class periods

PURPOSE: To understand how some ancient people communicated and perpetuated their history, to demonstrate how pictographs were drawn in caves, to experience one part of the daily life of the Anasazi, to use found objects as tools of art, to express through drawing, to stimulate imagination through imagery.

PROCEDURES:

This particular unit of study focuses on the Anasazi, an ancient people of the southwestern part of the United States, who were cave dwellers and lived in areas surrounded by canyons. The following activities give the students an opportunity to become those ancient people, through experiences that those people might have experienced. The activities require imagination and mood. They are a way of making the information come alive.

WARM-UPS AND THE ANASAZI:

There are many children's and young adult books that beautifully illustrate the Native American culture of long ago and today. Some suggested titles are *I'm in Charge of Celebrations* and *It Is Still That Way* by Byrd Baylor, *The Legend of the Indian Paintbrush* by Tomie dePaola, *The Cave* by Elizabeth Coatsworth, and *The First Book of the Cliff Dwellers* by Rebecca Marcus.

To set the mood, play an appropriate selection of music such as *Canyon Trilogy* by R. Carlos Nakai or Paul Winter's *Canyon*. Play music throughout the unit, as it calms the students and creates a mood appropriate to the topic being studied. Ask the students to make themselves comfortable by sitting on the floor. Use this time to review what has been learned thus far about Native Americans or the Anasazi, and read one of the children's books as a focus for the upcoming creative arts activities.

PICTURE DICTIONARY AND THE ANCIENT PEOPLE:

1. Begin a discussion by defining the words *pictograph* and *petroglyphs*. Show pictures of different actual pictographs found on canyon walls or in caves. Have resource books such as *Ancient Indians of the Southwest* by Alfred Tamarin and Shirley Glubok or *Anasazi and Pueblo Painting* by J. J. Brody available for the class to look through to get an idea of what the actual cave art looks like.

---

2. Show samples of different symbols used in these drawings. Picture dictionaries of ancient symbols can be obtained at local libraries or in social studies texts. Now give each student a sheet of paper that has a list of the following words on it:

sun	deer	fish
rain	river	bear
sky	mountains	fire
clouds	eagle	maize
happy	good	pottery
sad	bad	adobe
moon	star	baskets
man	drum	gourds
woman		

3. On the chalkboard, write the word *sun*. Ask different students to come to the board and draw their own symbol for the word.

4. Let students draw one symbol for each of the words that are on the sheet of paper.

IMAGERY AND THE ANASAZI:

1. Dim the lights and ask students to find a comfortable spot. In a slow, careful voice, present the story on page 206 through imagery form. Ask the students to relax, take a few breaths, close their eyes, and just listen as their mind takes them on an adventure.

The Cave

by Martha Brady

It is freezing now. The wind has come riding down from the north and turned all of the land around me into hard, cold earth. When I walk through the canyon walls, I must wrap what clothing I am wearing tightly around me, so that the bitter cold does not seep into my body. For if it does, I will die as so many others of my family have.

I walk down the canyon path remembering the spring and the warm days that spread under the warm sun. I remember the grasses, the trees, the berries. I long for the waterfalls rushing down from high atop the cliffs and into a beautiful green basin below. I long to lie underneath the blanket of stars and chant the chant of my elders. I long for warmth. But there is none.

I continue walking along the path, watching where my feet take me, careful, lest I should stumble from the numbness of my toes and fall over the edge of the canyon. I have a pouch tied around my waist. In it are sticks and rocks and some dried leaves bound together with animal sinew. In the pouch also are dyes saved from the summer, yellow dye made form the rabbit brush I find near my home, black dye made from boiling the stems of the bee plant, and red dye, my favorite, made from the alder bark and the roots of the mahogany tree. These are special things in my pouch, special things I have saved over the last few months. Special things that will allow me to once again paint in the cave.

The trail levels off now, and I walk for a good distance on flat ground. Suddenly I see it up above, near the ledge. I hold onto some large jagged boulders that are sticking out of the side of the canyon wall. I climb among the boulders and find myself at the entrance of a cave.

Even though it is still day, it is dark inside, and still, and very very cold. The shadows move along the walls of the cave, making pictures of their own. With my pouch I walk in. I shiver, pull my animal skin closer around me, and think of the summer warmth. Of the laughter, the singing, and the dancing the summer brings.

I walk further into the cave until the blackness requires me to stop. I look around at the slick walls, and I find a clean spot where I can tell my story. My mind is full of so many stories, of fish found in the river that ribbons through the canyon, of the basket weaving around the warm fires, of the game that is so elusive now. I think of the hardship of finding enough to eat. I think of my brothers who went to the top of the canyon and beyond, never to return. I think of so many things, here in this dark, still cave. And I wrap the animal skin even tighter around me and begin to tell my story.

CAVE ART AND THE ANASAZI:

To make the following activity even more meaningful, we would suggest setting this up in advance in another room so the students are not aware of it. It is very important that once "The Cave" has been told, the class goes immediately into this activity.

1. Ask students to go to the playground and find something to use as a paintbrush, such as a rock, a stick, or a bunch of weeds held together with a rubber band.

2. Before reading "The Cave," tape long sheets of brown or tan butcher paper along the lower portions of the walls. Students will be sitting while they draw. Cover the floor well with newspapers to prevent drips.

3. Play some appropriate Native American flute music. (R. Carlos Nakai is a Navajo musician who has several tapes on the market. These excellent tapes are produced on the Canyon label.)

4. Place flashlights in strategic places around the butcher papered walls to set the mood of shadows and darkness, and to give the room a cave-like effect.

5. After reading "The Cave" bring the class to this room, which will be lit only by the few flashlights placed here and there. Using the brush that they found on the playground, students will begin to tell a story by drawing on the cave walls.

6. At the conclusion of this activity, lead a discussion and sharing session about the students' feelings during the activity, the difficulty in using primitive tools, and the stories that were told on the cave walls.

MOVEMENT AND THE ANASAZI:

1. Once the students have had a chance to share the stories they painted on the cave walls, give them a chance to tell the stories in a different way, through movement.

2. Stretch a light, plain colored sheet over a piece of string that has been stretched across the corner of the room. Refer to the Shadow Puppet exercise in the "Puppetry" chapter of this book (pp. 90-91). The light source for this shadow stage can be a filmstrip projector or a couple of clip-on lights.

3. As one student is telling the painted story, another student is depicting that story through shadow movement behind the screen. Keep the flute music going even through this part of the activity.

Appendix

NUTS & BOLTS

nuts (nuts) *n.* 1: little things that are interesting.
bolts (bōlts) *n.* 1: flashes of lightning.
nuts and bolts (nuts and bōlts) *n.* 1: flashes of interesting things 2: how, when, and where 3: loose ends 4: what you need to make it work 5: appendix 6: ideas 7: fun.

Catalogs

American Science and Surplus
601 Linden Pl.
Evanston, IL 60202
(708) 475-8440

Masks, plastic bottles, gigantic plastic bags, balloons, Day-Glo adhesive tape, plastic animals, rubber balls, buttons, and more.

Anderson's
White Bear Lake, MN 55110
(800) 328-9640

Balloons, streamers, cellophane, decorator tape, corrugated paper, photo murals, party hats, leis, Hawaiian accessories, Japanese accessories, key chains, pom-poms, and more.

General Music Store
50741 U.S. Hwy. 33 North
South Bend, IN 46637

Percussion instruments, recorders, Autoharps.

National Music Supply
P.O. Box 14421
St. Petersburg, FL 33773

All kinds of percussion instruments, recorders, Autoharps, music stands.

National Supply Company
P.O. Box 3147
Sioux City, IA 51102
(712) 277-7070

Streamer crepe, crepe rolls, metallic streamers, corrugated wall trimming, drawing paper, paints, sign supplies, balloons, hats, crowns, pom-poms, garlands, and much more.

Norcostco
P.O. Box 22597
Minneapolis, MN 55422

Costumes, wigs, sound effects, hats, dance wear, hand props, paint, clown supplies, sound and lighting accessories and much more.

Oriental Trading Company, Inc.
P.O. Box 3407
Omaha, NE 68103
(800) 228-2269
(800) 535-7335

Stuffed animals, balloons, gag and trick items, school day specials, musical toys, hats, luau decorations, wigs, makeup, Halloween decorations, Christmas decorations, masks, and much more.

Rhythm Band Inc.
P.O. Box 126
Ft. Worth, TX 76101

Rhythm band instruments for all ages.

Theatre House, Inc.
400 W. Third St.
Covington, KY 41012
(606) 431-2414

Costumes, mustaches, makeup, beards, fabrics, spangle braids, headwear, dance wear, masks, stage weapons, gloves, stage accessories, crepe paper, posters, backdrops, sound effect albums, mood music, Christmas supplies, and much more.

Publishing Houses for Children's Musicals and Plays

Baker's Plays
100 Chauncy St.
Boston, MA 02111

Clarus Music, Ltd.
340 Bellevue Ave.
Yonkers, NY 10703

Contemporary Drama Service
P.O. Box 7710
Colorado Springs, CO 80933

Pioneer Drama Service, Inc.
2172 S. Colorado Blvd.
Denver, CO 80222

PLAYS, Inc.
120 Boylston St.
Boston, MA 02116

Popplers
123 Demers Ave.
Grand Forks, ND 58206

Reader's Theatre Script Service
P.O. Box 178333
San Diego, CA 97117

Bibliography

Birkenshaw, Lois. *Music for Fun, Music for Learning.* St. Louis, Mo.: MagnaMusic-Baton, Inc., 1982.

Boorman, Joyce. *Creative Dance in Grades Four to Six.* Don Mills, Ont.: Academic Press, 1969.

_____. *Creative Dance in the First Three Grades.* Don Mills, Ont.: Academic Press, 1969.

Freericks, Mary, and Joyce Segal. *Creative Puppetry in the Classroom.* Rowayton, Conn.: New Plays Books, 1979.

Goodwillie, Barbara. *Breaking Through.* Rowayton, Conn.: New Plays Books, 1986.

Heinig, Ruth. *Creative Drama for the Classroom.* Englewood Cliffs, N.J.: Prentice-Hall, 1988.

Hendricks, Gay, and Katheryn Hendricks. *The Moving Center.* Englewood Cliffs: N.J.: Prentice-Hall, 1983.

Kaplan, Don. *See with Your Ears.* San Francisco: Lexicos, 1983.

Kay, Drina. *All the Desk's a Stage.* Nashville, Tenn.: Incentive, 1982.

Mandell, Muriel, and Robert E. Wood. *Make Your Own Musical Instruments.* New York: Sterling, 1957.

Nobleman, Roberta. *Mime and Masks.* Rowayton, Conn.: New Plays Books, 1979.

Owens, Fred. *Theatre Games.* San Francisco: Diamond Heights, 1975.

Scher, Anna, and Charles Verrall. *100+ Ideas for Drama.* Hollywood, Calif.: Samuel French, 1975.

Spolin, Viola. *Theater Games for the Classroom.* Evanston, Ill.: Northwestern University Press, 1986.

Tanner, Fran Everett. *Basic Drama Projects.* Pocatello, Idaho: Clark, 1966.

Weikart, Phyllis. *Teaching Movement and Dance.* Ypsilanti, Mich.: Scope Press, 1982.

_____. *Whistles and Strings.* Newton, Mass.: Educational Developmental Center, 1968.

Index

About
the Authors

Martha Brady has been an educator for the past 25 years, as an elementary teacher and a middle school fine arts magnet coordinator in Texas, a performing arts specialist in Colorado, and currently as an instructor at Northern Arizona University, Flagstaff, Arizona, where she teaches creative arts courses and supervises student teachers.

A nationally known presenter and creative arts consultant, Ms. Brady travels across the nation giving arts integration workshops to elementary faculties, special education teachers, and reading specialists. She is also a member of the Arizona Department of Education Fine Arts Cadre and a faculty member of the Early Childhood Academy of Arizona.

Ms. Brady's children's musicals and children's songs are presented in schools throughout the Southwest.

Patsy Gleason has been an educator at all levels of academic learning for the past 20 years. She has been an elementary teacher, an assistant fine arts specialist in Colorado, an assistant professor in Northern Arizona University's elementary education teacher training program, an assistant principal in an inner city elementary/magnet middle school, and currently is a director of curriculum and instruction. Dr. Gleason is active in supporting the integration of the arts into current educational practices and daily classroom learning.